BIBLICAL ADVANCED BASICS
book one

UNDERSTANDING *the*

BIBLE
END
TIMES

FREDERICK E. LEWIS

REDEMPTION
PRESS

Re-Published in 2017 by Redemption Press, PO Box 427, Enumclaw, WA 98022 Toll Free (844) 2REDEEM (273-3336)

Redemption Press is honored to present this title in partnership with the author. The views expressed or implied in this work are those of the author. Redemption Press provides our imprint seal representing design excellence, creative content and high quality production.

Unless otherwise noted, all Scripture quotations are taken from the *Holy Bible, King James Version*, Cambridge, 1769.

ISBN: 978-1-68314-548-6

DEDICATION

This book is dedicated to my family, who were the only ones I had planned to share this information with initially. Without the patience and support of my loving wife, Jan, I could have lost my way on many occasions.

ACKNOWLEDGMENT

I wish to acknowledge Rollin E. Wilson, Jr., who went home to be with the Lord in May 2002, at the age of 70. I had the good fortune of knowing Rollin for ten years before he died. He was a pastor of numerous churches over nearly a fifty-year period, authored two books, and composed many Bible studies. I had an opportunity to study with him for those ten years and he always encouraged me to write down and organize what I was learning. One time, after many months of study, I took a brand-new Bible and read it through while highlighting every verse that brought up a question in my mind. I then went to a Bible computer program and downloaded every verse and printed a copy, which I placed in a three-ring binder. Over the next several weeks, Rollin went through every verse with me and answered every question I had about them. For this I will be eternally grateful. Thanks, Rollin, for everything. I look forward to seeing you again in *that day.*

TABLE OF CONTENTS

PREFACE

Permit me to preface this book with part of my personal story. I was raised in a Baptist Church and Jan, my wife of over forty years, in a Lutheran Church. When we were first married we would alternate between the two churches as we lived in the same city in which we grew up. After a stint in the military, the children started to come and we visited new churches to find a single church home. This went on for about twelve years and during that time I began to have an interest in studying about End Times, known as *eschatology.*

During the late 70's, I read a book by Hal Lindsey titled *Late Great Planet Earth* and it was helpful in kindling my interest. As I would try to study in the various churches we visited, I discovered that there was a wide variety of opposing views concerning what the Bible taught about End Times. I was still a few years away from coming to a knowledge of the *mystery* given to the Apostle Paul by direct revelation from the Lord Jesus Christ.

Basically, I found two main systems of theology, covenant and dispensational. Covenant theology centers around the belief that God has but one overall program in dealing with us and tends to spiritualize many passages that the dispensationalists take as literal. Dispensational theology includes a belief that God has changed the program from time to time in dealing with us.

On the covenant side you have amillennialism, where it's believed that the kingdom promised to Israel is occurring now in the spiritual realm, and there isn't to be a literal earthly kingdom set up in the future. Under this covenant system there would be no *rapture* of the church prior to the end and the majority of the events of the book of Revelation are taken to be fulfilled in a spiritual setting only. Jan's upbringing in the Lutheran Church embraces this type of interpretation.

The dispensationalists, on the other hand, believe in a literal earthly kingdom established after the *rapture* of the church and the period of time known as the *tribulation,* when the events of the book of Revelation will be literally played out. My Baptist upbringing embraces this type of interpretation.

As I was wrestling with trying to sort out the above, some friends invited Jan and me to their baptismal ceremony as they were joining a new church. At that service we met the preacher of their new church, which turned out to be a non-denominational church on the covenant side of interpretation. We ended up joining that church in the early 1980's. The preacher was a great teacher and we had a good-sized Bible study that met each week for years. Without that Bible study I would never have learned how the covenant side worked.

As I studied I realized that what I was learning was very different from what I was taught growing up, but I couldn't seem to find a way to understand what the Bible really taught on End Times and many other issues. For example, I was water baptized by immersion when I was ten years old after making a public statement that I wanted to trust Christ for my salvation. Jan, on the other hand, was water baptized by sprinkling as an infant. The new church believed that water baptism by immersion was a necessary act for anyone wanting to trust Christ for salvation and Jan and the children were all water baptized in this fashion (the children were also water baptized by sprinkling as infants).

After about five years at the new church, I had studied about everything I could get my hands on regarding End Times and many other topics. At this time I began reading the Bible through cover to cover to see if I could figure out which system of interpretation fit the Scriptures.

A friend of mine, Dave, called me one day about one to two years after my starting to read the Bible on a daily basis. He said he had an idea he wanted to run by me. When we were together he seemed more serious than I usually saw him. He said he had something to share and he didn't know with whom else he could share it. Over the years, he and I had talked extensively concerning matters of the Bible, and through the Bible studies we both attended he came to know the Lord.

He related a story to me that took him back to his younger schooldays. As the story went he had run away from home, due to a disagreement, by hitchhiking from Michigan to Indiana. On one of the rides he received, somehow his wallet worked its way out of his pocket and was undiscovered by Dave until it was too late. Through a series of events his father drove down to pick him up and he was homeward bound still with no wallet. After being back home for a few days a package arrived containing his missing wallet. It turned out that the driver was a local pastor, who found the wallet, was able to get an address from its contents, and mail the wallet back to him along with a Bible tract titled, *Simple As Can Be* by Cornelius Stam. Dave was delighted to get the wallet back and took the tract, without reading it, and zipped it into the Bible he had received when he was confirmed a few years before at his local church.

After more than twenty years, and during a move to a different house, the zippered Bible showed itself and Dave realized that he hadn't opened that Bible in over twenty years. When he did the Bible tract popped out and this time he read it and called me for the meeting mentioned earlier. Our conversation over lunch centered on the concepts in that tract, which outlined a system of Bible interpretation that takes into consideration the idea that God changed the program of his dealings with mankind about midway through the book of Acts. At that point God essentially concluded the kingdom program temporarily and ushered in a new program, known as the *mystery*, through the Apostle Paul. The complete changeover to the new program took about thirty years as Paul was receiving direct revelations concerning the new program from the ascended Lord Jesus Christ. This system of Bible interpretation is dispensational except it recognizes that the current church, the body of Christ, began in the mid part of the book of Acts and not, as most view its start, in the first part of Acts. The significance of the mid-Acts position is that the truth of the distinctive message and ministry of the Apostle Paul is recovered. When you view his letters as such, all the confusion disappears that occurs when you mix the previous kingdom program with the current one, communicated to him, known as the *mystery*. It took some time to discover the broad and sweeping nature of this new program, but it has led me to a much clearer understanding of topics such as End Times and others.

Since that meeting I have read the Bible through numerous times, in many versions, and have spent hundreds of hours in intense study to be able to come to a better understanding of many biblical topics. It is from this backdrop that I submit the following:

INTRODUCTION

Part 1 – *Simple As Can Be* by Cornelius R. Stam

(Bible tract mentioned above reprinted by permission)

Part 2 – Confusion in the Church Today

Part 3 – A Trip through the Bible

Part 4 – A Biblical Look at End Times

INTRODUCTION

An obvious question would be: "Why do we need another book about the Bible, hasn't there been enough written already?" Well, at one time I started reading some of those books in order to help with the goal of understanding End Times. What I discovered was mass confusion followed by frustration on my part. It seems that there is a very high interest in the topic of End Times and a vacuum like that will always draw a multitude of thought. Much of that thought has been published at one time or another, and therein lies the problem. In order to be able to sort through the confusion with a measure of objectivity, and to make some sense of the End Times topic, I recommend the following five steps:

1. Discover, catalog, and evaluate the various thought offerings on the topic.
2. Read the entire Bible through (more than once) with the idea (and prayer) that God's Word will speak to you and reveal the proper understanding.
3. Record your thoughts in a daily journal first and then collect those thoughts and insights into a treatise that summarizes what you learn on your way.
4. Have discussions with trusted advisors who can add to the depth of your overall concepts and understanding.
5. Finally, publish or print and share your results

to expose your work to a broader group for critique.

Granted, most people will never go to the trouble of the above process. I think the main reason for this is that it is commonly thought that the Bible is such a difficult book that you must attend a seminary for many years to be able to come to a proper understanding of Scripture. However, if that were true, today's confusion wouldn't exist amid all the schools of theology that are out there and are well attended.

One main theme of this book is that the Bible can be understood and you don't need a PhD for that to happen. In fact, a PhD may be detrimental to a sincere desire to understand many of the topics in God's Word. The reason is that, historically, entire systems of interpretation have been developed over the years and any errors have been magnified by the sheer numbers of people influenced by a formalized educational system. In that setting one is not encouraged to challenge and correct a given scenario and the result is that there is very little new thought offered and incorporated. On the contrary, the educational format penalizes those who discover a different slant on the course material and rewards those who learn and accept a given system of thought with an A+ on the final exam.

My college years were back in the early sixties and as an English major, the courses I took didn't lend themselves to much debate. As a result I didn't personally then find opposition of the above kind. My son, however, studied Economics in the late nineties and faced opposition due to his challenging much of what he was being taught. Needless to say, in a spirit of trying to learn, he was made to feel uncomfortable for not readily accepting all the course material. On one occasion he stayed after class to pursue a particular area with the professor, and after winning out with his point of view, was told by the professor that the course couldn't be corrected accordingly because of the flack he would receive from higher up. I believe this same thing has been going on since man was put on this earth by the Creator. It's part of the learning process.

This book is the result of my going through the steps above over about a twenty-year span of time. Over those years as I tested out what I was learning with various members of the clergy and laity, I experienced much opposition to any new thoughts I came across. Let me offer an example. One afternoon Jan and I were with friends at their house for their daughter's graduation party. There were many others in attendance from the church we all attended, which was mentioned in the Preface. At one point a man at the table I was sitting at made a reference to the future coming of Christ. I simply asked him: "How many more comings of Christ are there?" Immediately, another person at the table, supposedly a friend of mine, snapped: "Oh Fred, you've been reading too many books!" I tried to respond with gentleness (a little sarcasm crept in) and said: "Maybe so, but the Book I spend the most time in is called the *Bible*." The discussion abruptly ended when someone else changed the subject. Had a discussion ensued I would have had an excellent opportunity to share something about the *rapture* that will precede our Lord's Second Coming that I had learned and was excited about. The church body represented that afternoon didn't believe that there is going to be a *rapture,* and therefore the thought that there is going to be a Coming preceding and in addition to the Second Coming was considered heresy. I have learned that the average population out there doesn't want to enter into a discussion involving biblical concepts because it might take them out of the comfort zone of what they were taught. Any true seeker yearns for these types of discussions and many times is hard pressed to find them. It all goes back to what I said earlier, in that it isn't *politically correct* to challenge established thought.

Let me give you a word of encouragement, however. People can be wrong, about many things, much of the time. That is why we can't cap off truth and stop looking for light to be shed on any certain topic. There has always been opposition to truth in an endless tale of persecution and even death in some eras. Fortunately, we now live in a time setting, in our country, that doesn't involve *shooting the messenger*. At least, I hope (with a small grin on my face) that isn't the case. Seriously, there has always been and always will be resistance to anyone who *rocks the boat* with new and different ideas.

If a book can be called a journey, then this one would be a journey taken to understand what the Bible teaches about End Times. The journey begins with the thought that God put the prophetic program, and thus the kingdom church, on temporary hold in the mid part of the book of Acts. This one thought alone helped me to eliminate as error the written thought that looks to headlines in the newspapers for insight as to where we are in God's overall plan. If you will prayerfully read this entire book, in as few sittings as possible, I trust that the next time you read the Bible through you will be thrilled at how it will open up to you. I have endeavored to keep this book brief enough for it to be read (or reread) in two to three hours of time.

In Part 1, following this introduction, there is a reprint of the Bible tract, mentioned in the Preface, written over fifty years ago by a man who did: "**. . . earnestly contend for the faith which was once delivered to the saints**" (Jude 1:3). In that time setting there was fierce opposition to the "**. . . preaching of Jesus Christ according to the revelation of the mystery**" (Romans 16:25). As a result, the tract is a no-nonsense, hard-pounding treatise during a time of the recent recovery of: *the truth of the distinctive message and ministry of the Apostle Paul*. I will offer a chronicled chart of this and other truths lost and recovered in Part 2.

One final thought before we begin our journey: "All the Bible is for us, but it is not all addressed to us or written about us, and if we would really understand and enjoy it; if we would really know how to use it effectively in service for Christ, we must be careful always to note who is addressing whom, about what and when and why."[1]

Let's begin our study.

---

[1] Cornelius R. Stam, *Things That Differ,* page 20.

PART 1

SIMPLE AS CAN BE

by Cornelius R. Stam
Used by permission.[2]

Yes, the plan of salvation is simple *if* the Scriptures are rightly divided. Otherwise it is far from simple. Hence the grave responsibility upon those engaged in the work of the Lord to obey II Timothy 2:15:

"Study to shew thyself approved unto God, a workman that needeth not to be ashamed, rightly dividing the word of truth."

Let us illustrate:

Here in the heart of a city, let us say, stands a man who has been convicted of his sin. He is miserable as, at last, he sees himself as he really is, a guilty, condemned sinner.

As he stands there brooding, Mr. Average Fundamentalist comes walking down the street. In his lapel he has a button which reads "Jesus Saves." Seeing this our unsaved friend thinks, "Here is the man for me," and approaching him says, "I wonder if you can help me. I'm in trouble. What must I do to be saved?"

---

[2] Berean Bible Society, for additional literature: (262)255-4750, www.bereanbiblesociety.org

"Why!" exclaims Mr. Average Fundamentalist, "I'm so glad you ask me. There are some things in the Bible which are hard to understand but, thank God, the way of salvation is as simple as can be. Look here in my New Testament at Acts 16:30,31. When the Philippian jailor asked the same question Paul answered: **"Believe on the Lord Jesus Christ, and thou shalt be saved"**

Isn't that simple! That's all you need to do. Just believe on the Lord Jesus Christ and salvation is yours. And here are a few more Scriptures along the same line:

John 3:36: **"He that believeth on the Son hath everlasting life: and he that believeth not the Son shall not see life; but the wrath of God abideth on him."**

Romans 4:5: **"But to him that worketh not, but believeth on him that justifieth the ungodly, his faith is counted for righteousness."**

Ephesians 2:8,9: **"For by grace are ye saved through faith; and that not of yourselves: *it is* the gift of God: Not of works, lest any man should boast."**

But while Mr. Average Fundamentalist has been showing our friend the simple plan of salvation a Roman Catholic has been listening to the conversation. At last he can contain himself no longer. Stepping up to Mr. Fundamentalist he says, "Pardon me for interrupting, sir, but you are leading this man astray. Don't you know that James 2:20 says that:" **"Faith without works is dead"** "And I dare you to read James 2:24 to this man." Turning to the passage Mr. Fundamentalist reads: **"Ye see then how that by works a man is justified, and not by faith only."**

"Could anything be plainer than that?" says the Roman Catholic; and with this he begins to outline all those works which he considers necessary to salvation. Just then a *Campbellite* steps up and says, "I've been listening to you gentlemen and if you will pardon me I think Mr. Fundamentalist is making salvation too easy while our Catholic friend here is making it too hard. It shouldn't be difficult to determine what is required for salvation, for our Lord Himself made it very plain when He commissioned His apostles to preach the gospel. Look, here in Mark 16:15,16 we have it as simple as can be:

"And he said unto them, Go ye into all the world, and preach the gospel to every creature. He that believeth and is baptized shall be saved; but he that believeth not shall be damned."

"Isn't that plain? If this Scripture means anything, then those who believe and are baptized and those alone, are saved. And notice how carefully Peter carried out this commission at Pentecost. When his hearers were convicted of their guilt and began to ask what they must do to be saved, what did he say to them?"

Acts 2:38: "Then Peter said unto them, Repent, and be baptized every one of you in the name of Jesus Christ for the remission of sins, and ye shall receive the gift of the Holy Ghost."

"It seems to me that anyone who really wants to know the truth should see that, - it's so simple." But now a Pentecostalist steps into the circle, almost exploding: "Why didn't you read those next verses in Mark 16, Mr. Campbellite? Why did you stop right in the middle of the passage? The rest is plain too, only you won't receive it. See what it says here:"

Mark 16:17,18: **"And these signs shall follow them that believe; In my name shall they cast out devils; they shall speak with new tongues;**

"They shall take up serpents; and if they drink any deadly thing, it shall not hurt them; they shall lay hands on the sick, and they shall recover."

"Isn't that perfectly plain?

"So according to the same *Great Commission,* if you do not have miraculous powers you are not a true believer. You can't make it mean anything else, for it distinctly says:" **"these signs shall follow them that believe;"**

"None of you can deny that under the *Great Commission,* which practically all Christians claim to follow, faith and water baptism are the requirements for salvation while miraculous powers are the evidences of salvation."

Finally one more person joins the company, saying, "Haven't you men all forgotten something?"

"What?" they all ask.

"Why, apparently you have forgotten that there is an Old Testament in the Bible! And the Old Testament is three times as large as the New!"

The speaker is a Seventh Day Adventist, and he presses his point home:

"Don't you know the terms of God's holy law? Let's turn to Exodus 19:5 and see what it says:"

"Now therefore, if ye will obey my voice indeed, and keep my covenant, then ye shall be a peculiar treasure unto me above all people: for all the earth *is* mine:"

With Scripture after Scripture the Seventh Day Adventist seeks to prove that the observance of the ten commandments is essential to acceptance with God. Especially does he stress sabbath observance as the very sign of relationship to God. To prove this he quotes Exodus 31:13 and 17:

"Speak thou also unto the children of Israel, saying, Verily my sabbaths ye shall keep: for it *is* **a sign between me and you throughout your generations; that** *ye* **may know that I** *am* **the LORD that doth sanctify you. It** *is* **a sign between me and the children of Israel for ever . . ."**

Poor, unsaved man!

All this began with his simple question: "What must I do to be saved?"

Mr. Fundamentalist's plan had seemed so simple until the others had begun challenging him, - and each other. And strangely each of the others seemed to think his particular view was "so simple" too!

But our poor unsaved friend! What can he make of all this as he stands there, guilty and condemned? Certainly the way to peace doesn't seem very simple to him now.

And no man had better say the plan of salvation is simple if he does not "rightly divide the Word of truth."

No man had better say it is simple who claims to be working under the *Great Commission.*

No man had better say it is simple who teaches that Pentecost marked the beginning of the Body of Christ, the Church of this age.

No man had better say it is simple who denies the distinctive ministry of the Apostle Paul. The way of salvation for sinners today can only be simple when we recognize our place in history and acknowledge that to Paul, by special revelation, God made known His message for the world *today* and His program for the Church *today.*

It should surely seem significant to the careful student of Scripture that after our Lord had given the *Great Commission* to His apostles, another apostle, Paul, should dare to say:

Romans 11:13: **"For I speak to you Gentiles, inasmuch as I am the apostle of the Gentiles, I magnify mine office:"**

Did God then raise up Paul because the twelve were unfaithful in carrying out the *Great Commission?* Indeed not. It was Israel's rejection of the kingdom message and God's infinite grace to a lost world that brought about the conversion and commission of Paul.

See Paul's own words to the Jews at Antioch in Pisidia, some years later:

Acts 13:46: **"Then Paul and Barnabas waxed bold, and said, It was necessary that the word of God should first have been spoken to you: but seeing ye put it from you, and judge yourselves unworthy of everlasting life, lo, we turn to the Gentiles."**

We have but to read Galatians 2 to learn that it was by the will of God and under the direction of the Holy Spirit that the leaders of the twelve finally handed over their Gentile ministry to Paul who went to them with another message, **"That gospel which I preach among the Gentiles,"** **"The gospel of the grace of God."** (Read carefully Galatians 2:1–10).

We must not forget that when Israel rejected the glorified King and His Kingdom, the last and only nation which still had a relationship with God was alienated from Him. The very channel of God's blessing to the nations (Genesis 22:17,18) was stopped up, as it were.

Romans 5:20: **"Moreover the law entered, that the offence might abound. But where sin abounded, grace did much more abound:"**

In the crisis God acted to make known His eternal purpose in Christ, raising up Paul to proclaim the glorious news that in response to Israel's rebellion He would dispense grace to a world of lost sinners.

Salvation to the Gentiles through the fall of Israel! What grace! The favored nation temporarily cast out that individuals everywhere might find peace with God through the blood of the cross. See what Paul writes to the Gentiles in Romans 11:30–33:

"For as ye in times past have not believed God, yet have now obtained mercy through their unbelief: Even so have these also now not believed, that through your mercy they also may obtain mercy. For God hath concluded them all in unbelief, that he might have mercy upon all. O the depth of the riches both of the wisdom and knowledge of God! how unsearchable *are* his judgments, and his ways past finding out!"

God is having mercy upon all today and RECONCILING both Jews and Gentiles unto Himself in ONE BODY by the cross.

Ephesians 2:16: **"And that he might reconcile both unto God in one body by the cross, having slain the enmity thereby:"**

Salvation has come to the Gentiles, then, not through Israel's instrumentality but through her obstinacy, - not according to any covenant but by grace, - not through the ministry of the twelve, who were (and are) to be Israel's rulers (Matthew 19:28) but through the ministry of Paul, the rebel who **"obtained mercy."**

And so it is that in the eleventh chapter of Romans Paul emphasizes his commission as the apostle of the Gentiles. Read it again, and remember that it is not merely Paul's word. It is God's Word through Paul:

Romans 11:13: **"For I speak to you Gentiles, inasmuch as I am the apostle of the Gentiles, I magnify mine office:"**

If this does not satisfy the reader as to Paul's distinctive ministry to the Gentiles and his God-given authority as the Apostle of grace, surely no more should be needed than the opening verses of Ephesians 3:

Ephesians 3:1–3: **"For this cause I Paul, the prisoner of Jesus Christ for you Gentiles, If ye have heard of the dispensation of the grace of God which is given me to youward: How that by revelation he made known unto me the mystery; (as I wrote afore in few words."**

So important is this matter that even before the sentence of judgment was pronounced upon Israel and the kingdom hopes of that generation were fully withdrawn, Paul, with double emphasis, pronounced a curse upon any who dared to proclaim anything but the gospel of the grace of God to the Gentiles.

Galatians 1:8,9: **"But though we, or an angel from heaven, preach any other gospel unto you than that which we have preached unto you, let him be accursed. As we said before, so say I now again, If any *man* preach any other gospel unto you than that ye have received, let him be accursed."**

How these words should cause every sincere man of God to tremble and to make sure that his message conforms with that which the Lord of glory, from His throne in heaven, revealed to Paul!

Observe this and the plan of salvation is simple!

Do you ever find Paul proclaiming salvation by works? Does he ever command sabbath keeping, circumcision or water baptism? Not once. True, he practiced all of these during his early ministry, but that is what he came out of, - what he emerged from. Paul lived in a transition period. He was saved under the Jewish economy but raised up to bring in a new dispensation, - the dispensation of the grace of God.

And, note well, Paul was raised up to make known the very **"mystery** (secret) **of the gospel."** (Ephesians 6:19). When all mankind had demonstrated its utter sinfulness, God saved Saul of Tarsus, making known through him the riches of His grace, - showing how it was that anyone ever had been saved! Now it was revealed that it had not been the blood of beasts, the waters of baptism or any other physical ceremony that had saved the saints of ages past (though these were required under law) but the infinite grace of a loving God.

Read Paul's majestic words to the Romans:

> Romans 3:21–28: **"But now the righteousness of God without the law is manifested, being witnessed by the law and the prophets; Even the righteousness of God *which* is by faith of Jesus Christ unto all and upon all them that believe: for there is no difference: For all have sinned, and come short of the glory of God; Being justified freely by his grace through the redemption that is in Christ Jesus: Whom God hath set forth *to be* a propitiation through faith in his blood, to declare his righteousness for the remission of sins**

that are past, through the forbearance of God; To declare, *I say,* at this time his righteousness: that he might be just, and the justifier of him which believeth in Jesus. Where is boasting then? It is excluded. By what law? of works? Nay: but by the law of faith. Therefore we conclude that a man is justified by faith without the deeds of the law."

Yes, see this and the plan is sublimely simple. Today, NO works are required for salvation. Indeed salvation is offered to those who will stop working to get it, for today God wants us to see and acknowledge our utter ruin and His infinite grace.

Romans 4:4,5: "Now to him that worketh is the reward not reckoned of grace, but of debt. But to him that worketh not, but believeth on him that justifieth the ungodly, his faith is counted for righteousness."

Romans 5:1: "Therefore being justified by faith, we have peace with God through our Lord Jesus Christ:"

Titus 3:4,5: "But after that the kindness and love of God our Saviour toward man appeared, Not by works of righteousness which we have done, but according to his mercy he saved us, by the washing of regeneration, and renewing of the Holy Ghost;"

Ephesians 2:8–10: "For by grace are ye saved through faith; and that not of yourselves: *it is* the gift of God: Not of works, lest any man should boast. For we are his workmanship, created in Christ Jesus unto good works, which God hath before ordained that we should walk in them."

Ephesians 1:6,7: "To the praise of the glory of his grace, wherein he hath made us accepted in the beloved. In whom we have redemption through his blood, the forgiveness of sins, according to the riches of his grace;"

Colossians 2:9,10: "For in him dwelleth all the fulness of the Godhead bodily. And ye are complete in him, which is the head of all principality and power."

PART 2

CONFUSION IN THE CHURCH TODAY

In II Timothy 1:15 the Apostle Paul writes: **"This thou knowest, that all they which are in Asia be turned away from me; of whom are Phygellus and Hermogenes."** It was at that time that the distinctive message and ministry of the Apostle Paul began to be lost. This plunged the Christian church into a downward spiral that resulted in the further loss of: the truth of the pre-tribulational rapture of the church the body of Christ; the difference between Israel and the church the body of Christ; and the truth of justification by faith alone, in Christ alone. Over twenty years earlier Luke wrote in Acts 13:39 a quotation from a sermon by the Apostle Paul concerning justification: **"And by Him everyone who believes is justified from all things from which you could not be justified by the law of Moses."** Some historians have concluded that the loss of these truths contributed in a major way to bringing in the historical period called *the dark ages*.

It is suggested by the chart below that these truths were lost in a particular order and that they were recovered in reverse order:

Pauline Truths Lost (Order of Loss)[3]

First: *The Distinctive Message and Ministry of Paul*
II Timothy 1:15

Second: *The Pre-Tribulational Rapture of the Church,
the Body of Christ*

Third: *The Difference between Israel and the Church,
the Body of Christ*

Fourth: *Justification by Faith Alone, in Christ Alone*
Acts 13:39

Pauline Truths Recovered (Order of Recovery)

First: *Justification by Faith Alone, in Christ Alone*
Recovered via Protestant Reformation in the
16th Century via Luther, et al

Second: *The Difference between Israel and the Church,
the Body of Christ*
Recovered in the 1800's via John Nelson
Darby, Ethelbert William Bullinger, Sir Robert
Anderson, et al

Third: *The Pre-Tribulational Rapture of the Church,
the Body of Christ*
Recovered in the 19th Century via John
Nelson Darby and included by C.I. Scofield in
his Reference Bible, published 1909

Fourth: *The Distinctive Message and Ministry of Paul*
Recovered from the middle 1900's via John C.
O'Hair, Charles F. Baker, Cornelius R. Stam, et al

---

[3] Grace Bible College, TH 414—(adapted excerpt from) *Studies in Dispensational Theology*, T. F. Conklin, Course Prof., Spring 1994

During this entire process of loss and recovery of these truths, we saw the formation of most all of the over 400 denominations that can be observed today. The total revelation, given to the Apostle Paul by the Lord Jesus Christ during Paul's ministry of approximately thirty years, is referred to as the *mystery*. A key point in understanding the *mystery* is that God began a new program at that time to deal with His creation. The former program, called the *prophetic* program or the *kingdom*, concerned the Jews first, was prophesied by the prophets, had an earthly hope and calling, and involved Twelve Apostles. We will see in the remainder of this book how this prophetic or kingdom program will be resumed after the current program has run its course. The current program, called the *mystery*, concerns the Jews and Gentiles alike, was not forecast in the prophetic Scriptures, was hid in God, has a heavenly hope and calling, and involves one Apostle, Paul. Understanding the *mystery* makes it possible to understand that there are no denominations in the Bible and each current denomination is unique based upon which parts of the previous program are combined with the current program. All of the differences of Bible interpretation can be linked to this improper combining of two separate programs of God. A basic tool then would be to divide the Bible into the two parts. The chart below will identify which books of the Bible are written about which program. (Note, the books of Acts and Hebrews are transitional from one program to the other.)

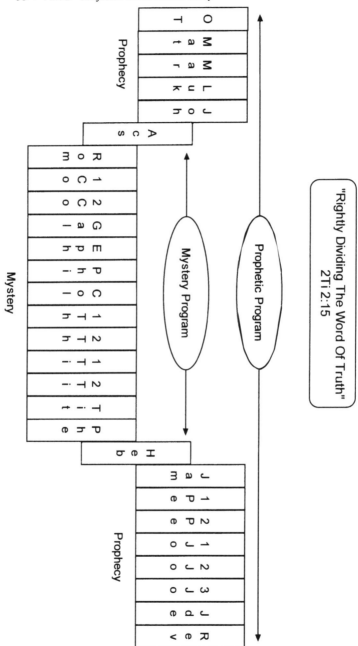

In II Timothy 2:15 we read: **"Study to shew thyself approved unto God, a workman that needeth not to be ashamed, rightly dividing the word of truth."** It is this principle of *right division* that makes it possible to understand the Bible amid all the denominational confusion. Remember what we read in I Corinthians 14:33: **"For God is not *the author* of confusion, but of peace, as in all the churches of the saints."** If Satan wants to confuse the body of Christ (and you better believe he does), what better way than to try to keep the members arguing over all the denominational differences that have accumulated over the years. I've heard it said that Romans 16:25: **". . . the preaching of Jesus Christ, according to the revelation of the mystery, which was kept secret since the world began,"** is Satan's worst nightmare and I believe this to be accurate. There is a passage in I Corinthians that points out that the **"princes of this world"** (or rulers, which would include physical as well as spiritual), would have done differently had they known the significance of the cross:

> 1 Corinthians 2:7,8: **"But we speak the wisdom of God in a mystery, *even* the hidden *wisdom*, which God ordained before the world unto our glory: Which none of the princes of this world knew: for had they known *it*, they would not have crucified the Lord of glory."**

With these four recovered truths in mind let's set aside all denominational considerations and tackle three of the most divisive questions in the church today: 1. *Baptism,* 2. *Eternal Security,* and 3. *Gifts of the Spirit.*

1. Baptism

Baptism as we see being used in many churches today began during the exodus of the Jews from Egypt before the giving of the Law. We read in Exodus 19:5,6 that if

Israel kept the covenant they would become a kingdom of priests. This is the first hint of the future kingdom that was spoken of later by the prophets. At the time of these verses, only specific members of the tribe of Levi could be eligible for the priesthood. Now, however, all Israel was given a conditional promise that they all could become priests in the future kingdom:

> Exodus 19:5,6: **"Now therefore, if ye will obey my voice indeed, and keep my covenant, then ye shall be a peculiar treasure unto me above all people: for all the earth *is* mine: And ye shall be unto me a kingdom of priests, and an holy nation. These *are* the words which thou shalt speak unto the children of Israel."**

This promise was later confirmed to Israel in the following verses:

> I Peter 2:9: **"But ye *are* a chosen generation, a royal priesthood, an holy nation, a peculiar people; that ye should shew forth the praises of him who hath called you out of darkness into his marvellous light."**

> Revelation 5:9,10: **" . . . Thou art worthy to take the book, and to open the seals thereof: for thou wast slain, and hast redeemed us to God by thy blood out of every kindred, and tongue, and people, and nation; And hast made us unto our God kings and priests: and we shall reign on the earth."**

> Revelation 20:6: **"Blessed and holy *is* he that hath part in the first resurrection: on such the second death hath no power, but they shall be priests of God and of Christ, and shall reign with him a thousand years."**

There was a blood and water ceremony required for the priests from the tribe of Levi to observe before being placed into the priesthood:

Exodus 29:1–4: **"And this *is* the thing that thou shalt do unto them to hallow them, to minister unto me in the priest's office: Take one young bullock, and two rams without blemish, And unleavened bread, and cakes unleavened tempered with oil, and wafers unleavened anointed with oil:** *of* **wheaten flour shalt thou make them. And thou shalt put them into one basket, and bring them in the basket, with the bullock and the two rams. And Aaron and his sons thou shalt bring unto the door of the tabernacle of the congregation, and shalt wash them with water."**

Exodus 29:10,11: **"And thou shalt cause a bullock to be brought before the tabernacle of the congregation: and Aaron and his sons shall put their hands upon the head of the bullock. And thou shalt kill the bullock before the LORD,** *by* **the door of the tabernacle of the congregation."**

Later in a prophecy by Ezekiel, Israel was told of a future day:

Ezekiel 36:24–28: **"For I will take you from among the heathen, and gather you out of all countries, and will bring you into your own land. Then will I sprinkle clean water upon you, and ye shall be clean: from all your filthiness, and from all your idols, will I cleanse you. A new heart also will I give you, and a new spirit will I put within you: and I will take away the stony heart out of your flesh, and I will give you an heart of flesh. And I will put my spirit within you, and cause you to walk in my statutes, and ye shall keep my**

judgments, and do *them*. And ye shall dwell in the land that I gave to your fathers; and ye shall be my people, and I will be your God."

It would appear that sprinkling was the method used in the water ceremony later to be known as baptism. Fast forward now to the time of John the Baptist and the preaching of the kingdom at hand. Israel was now ready to become that kingdom of priests if they would repent and submit to water baptism.

Matthew 3:1–6: **"In those days came John the Baptist, preaching in the wilderness of Judaea, And saying, Repent ye: for the kingdom of heaven is at hand. For this is he that was spoken of by the prophet Esaias, saying, The voice of one crying in the wilderness, Prepare ye the way of the Lord, make his paths straight. And the same John had his raiment of camel's hair, and a leathern girdle about his loins; and his meat was locusts and wild honey. Then went out to him Jerusalem, and all Judaea, and all the region round about Jordan, And were baptized of him in Jordan, confessing their sins."**

Matthew 4:17: **"From that time Jesus began to preach, and to say, Repent: for the kingdom of heaven is at hand."**

As you will see in Part 3, the majority in the nation Israel didn't repent and submit to water baptism. After the stoning of Stephen (the last straw), the kingdom program was temporarily set aside and the current program, called the *mystery,* was ushered in through the Apostle Paul. Water baptism has no part in the *mystery;* however, we are identified with, or baptized by, the Spirit into a new joint body called the body of Christ.

I Corinthians 12:13: **"For by one Spirit are we all baptized into one body, whether** *we be* **Jews or Gentiles, whether** *we be* **bond or free; and have been all made to drink into one Spirit."**

This is in accordance with the unity (i.e., the oneness) we have in Christ during the present program of God's grace. Here again, if we rightly divide the Scriptures, we see that whereas the kingdom program was replaced by the *mystery,* consequently water baptism was replaced by a Spirit(ual) baptism, or identification, with a new body, the body of Christ.

Ephesians 4:4–6: **"*There is* one body, and one Spirit, even as ye are called in one hope of your calling; One Lord, one faith, one baptism, One God and Father of all, who *is* above all, and through all, and in you all."**

2. Eternal Security

Moving next into the topic of eternal security (whether or not you can lose your salvation once saved), we look back in history to find that after the Protestant Reformation in the sixteenth century, this topic was among those that caused wars to be fought and men to be burned at the stake. It is certain that Satan didn't want truth to be rediscovered further than was already brought out by this Reformation (justification by faith alone, in Christ alone).

You will recall that the four truths, from the ministry of Paul, were lost for fifteen hundred years and recovered over a period of about three hundred and fifty years. During this whole process the multitude of confusion was due to not recognizing the distinctive message and ministry of the Apostle Paul (the last of the truths recovered). Without the principle of right division of the Scriptures, one is left in an incorrect *denominational* view based on which parts of the old kingdom program are mixed with the new *mystery* program.

God ushered in a new program of pure grace with that new apostle and many things changed. Where Israel had an earthly kingdom hope, we now have a heavenly calling and hope:

> Philippians 3:20,21: **"For our conversation** (Gr, *politeuma:* community, citizenship) **is in heaven; from whence also we look for the Saviour, the Lord Jesus Christ: Who shall change our vile body, that it may be fashioned like unto his glorious body, according to the working whereby he is able even to subdue all things unto himself."**

The terms of salvation in the former program were to repent and be water baptized for the remission of sins. The current program requires only that we believe in the death, burial, and resurrection of the Lord Jesus Christ and that He died for our sins:

> I Corinthians 15:1–4: **"Moreover, brethren, I declare unto you the gospel which I preached unto you, which also ye have received, and wherein ye stand; By which also ye are saved, if ye keep in memory what I preached unto you, unless ye have believed in vain. For I delivered unto you first of all that which I also received, how that Christ died for our sins according to the scriptures; And that he was buried, and that he rose again the third day according to the scriptures."**

There is nothing you can add to the work of Christ on the cross that will earn your salvation. By the same token there is nothing you can do after being saved to keep yourself saved. It is by grace and is a gift of God.

Some teach that once you are saved you can lose your salvation if you do certain things (or don't do certain things). This is a result of a failure to recognize that: Ephesians 2:8,9: **"For by grace are ye saved through faith; and that not of yourselves: *it is* a gift of God: not of works, lest any man should boast."** This passage goes on to say in the next verse: Ephesians 2:10: **"For we are his workmanship, created in Christ Jesus unto good works, which God hath before ordained that we should walk in them."** Good works are a result of being saved; being saved is not a result of good works. Simply put, you committed no sin so big that the cross of Christ couldn't pay the price to save you; and after being saved, there is no sin so big that the cross of Christ can't pay that price as well.

By mixing the two programs of God, many denominations tend to teach that we must do something to help earn our salvation, and likewise, we must do something to help keep it. The enemy can't make you lose your salvation, but if he can keep you uncertain of having it, then he can keep you from understanding the truth and seeking the spiritual growth you could otherwise gain.

Before we leave this important topic, let's search the Scriptures to see if one can be secure in Christ. There is one verse, one of the more familiar in the Bible, which pretty well says it all:

> John 3:16: **"For God so loved the world, that he gave his only begotten Son, that whosoever believeth in him should not perish, but have everlasting life."** In what sense is everlasting life everlasting, if you can lose it?

The next two verses add to the thought:

> John 3:17,18: **"For God sent not his Son into the world to condemn the world; but that the world through him might be saved. He that believeth on him is not condemned: but he that believeth not is condemned already, because he hath not believed in the name of the only begotten Son of God."**

In Hebrews 10:14 we read:

> **"For by one offering he hath perfected for ever them that are sanctified."**

Obviously, the above verses apply to the former as well as future kingdom program, but the topic of eternal security, like many other topics, can be trans-dispensational; that is, their truth is the same in any dispensation. Let's look to the Pauline record to see this truth for us:

> Romans 5:1: **"Therefore being justified by faith, we have peace with God through our Lord Jesus Christ."**

> Ephesians 1:13,14: **"In whom ye also *trusted,* after that ye heard the word of truth, the gospel of your salvation: in whom also after that ye believed, ye were sealed with that holy Spirit of promise, Which is the earnest of our inheritance until the redemption of the purchased possession, unto the praise of his glory."**

Once you have believed you are sealed with the Holy Spirit and that seal is stronger than the power of sin in your life.

Some object to the teaching of being eternally secure by observing that many so-called Christians seem to be as evil and as sin-ridden as non-believers. First of all, it is not for us to know for sure who is saved among us. Look at the example of Judas. He was one of the twelve and was an impostor, about whom Christ said in John 6:70, **" . . . Have not I chosen you twelve, and one of you is a devil?"** Secondly, even we as blood-bought, justified, and sealed believers will continue to sin due to our flesh, our sin nature. Let's verify this with a lamentation by the Apostle Paul himself:

> Romans 7:14–25: **"For we know that the law is spiritual: but I am carnal, sold under sin. For that which I do I allow not: for what I would, that do I not; but what I hate, that do I. If then I do that which I would not, I consent unto the law that *it is* good. Now then it is no more I that do it, but sin that dwelleth in me. For I know that in me (that is, in my flesh,) dwelleth no good thing: for to will is present with me; but *how* to perform that which is good I find not. For the good that I would I do not: but the evil which I would not, that I do. Now if I do that I would not, it is no more I that do it, but sin that dwelleth in me. I find then a law, that, when I would do good, evil is present with me. For I delight in the law of God after the inward man: But I see another law in my members, warring against the law of my mind, and bringing me into captivity to the law of sin which is in my members. O wretched man that I am! who shall deliver me from the body of this death? I thank God through Jesus Christ our Lord. So then with the mind I myself serve the law of God; but with the flesh the law of sin."**

We won't be rid of sin until we are caught up to be with Christ and evil is defeated once and for all.

Romans 6:23: **"For the wages of sin *is* death; but the gift of God *is* eternal life through Jesus Christ our Lord."**

Again, in what sense is eternal life eternal, if you can lose it?

Titus 3:5: **"Not by works of righteousness which we have done, but according to his mercy he saved us, by the washing of regeneration, and renewing of the Holy Ghost."**

Justice: getting what we deserve; *mercy:* not getting what we deserve; *grace:* getting what we don't deserve, praise God for His mercy and grace toward us by His love, through Christ!

Galatians 2:20: **"I am crucified with Christ: nevertheless I live; yet not I, but Christ liveth in me: and the life which I now live in the flesh I live by the faith of the Son of God, who loved me, and gave himself for me."**

Colossians 2:10–15: **"And ye are complete in him, which is the head of all principality and power: In whom also ye are circumcised with the circumcision made without hands, in putting off the body of the sins of the flesh by the circumcision of Christ: Buried with him in baptism, wherein also ye are risen with *him* through the faith of the operation of God, who hath raised him from the dead. And you, being dead in your sins and the uncircumcision of your flesh, hath he quickened together with him, having forgiven you all trespasses; Blotting out the handwriting of ordinances that was against us, which was contrary to us, and took it out of the way, nailing it to his cross; *And* having spoiled principalities**

and powers, he made a shew of them openly, triumphing over them in it."

I took the liberty of underlining the word *all* above and take it to mean *all* past, present, and future sins.

Romans 8:38,39: "For I am persuaded, that neither death, nor life, nor angels, nor principalities, nor powers, nor things present, nor things to come, Nor height, nor depth, nor any other creature, shall be able to separate us from the love of God, which is in Christ Jesus our Lord."

God wants us to know for sure that nothing can separate us from His love! The enemy would have you to believe that one or more certain types of sins will cause you to become separated from God's love.

Some denominations teach that we must confess our sins after being saved in order to have them forgiven. This is based on a verse from I John:

I John 1:9: "If we confess our sins, he is faithful and just to forgive us *our* sins, and to cleanse us from all unrighteousness."

Read that chapter *carefully*. First of all, this verse is addressing non-believers; and second of all, John was writing to Israel under the kingdom program, where they were to repent (and confess their sins), and be water baptized for their remission. In fact, during the tribulation, this same gospel of the kingdom will be preached in all the world, more on this later in Part 4.

Mark 1:4,5: "John did baptize in the wilderness, and preach the baptism of repentance for the remission of sins. And there went out unto him all the land of Judaea, and they of Jerusalem, and

were all baptized of him in the river of Jordan, confessing their sins."

3. Gifts of the Spirit

The gifts of the Spirit were primarily: words of wisdom, words of knowledge, gifts of healing, miracles, prophecy, discerning of spirits, tongues, and interpretation of tongues. Yes, it is true that in Paul's early ministry all these gifts were in operation and were practiced. As we have seen before, it took approximately thirty years for Paul to receive all the divine revelations from our Lord and write all his epistles.

> Acts 26:16: **"But rise, and stand upon thy feet: for I have appeared unto thee for this purpose, to make thee a minister and a witness both of these things which thou hast seen, and of those things in the which I will appear unto thee."**

> II Corinthians 12:1: **"It is not expedient for me doubtless to glory. I will come to visions and revelations of the Lord."**

In I Corinthians 13:8–10 we read:

> **"Charity never faileth: but whether *there be* prophecies, they shall fail; whether *there be* tongues, they shall cease; whether *there be* knowledge, it shall vanish away. For we know in part, and we prophesy in part. But when that which is perfect is come, then that which is in part shall be done away."**

During those years the Holy Spirit was supplementing the lack of the total revelation being revealed to Paul by the use of the gifts of the Spirit. As the last verse above states, **"when that which is perfect** (Gr, *teleios:* complete)[4] **is come, then that which is in part shall be done away."**

[4]Some would take this as meaning that when Christ returns in the *rapture,* the gifts will be done away. Neither the Greek word for *perfect,* which is neuter, nor the sentence structure supports this idea. We would have found "when He who is perfect" rather than "when that which is perfect."

It makes sense that when God was through inspiring the Scriptures to be written, there would no longer be a need to have more parts coming with the gifts of the Spirit. There is evidence that these gifts were already being withdrawn before the end of Paul's ministry.

II Corinthians 4:16: **"For which cause we faint not; but though our outward man perish, yet the inward *man* is renewed day by day."**

II Corinthians 5:2: **"For in this we groan, earnestly desiring to be clothed upon with our house which is from heaven."**

II Corinthians 12:7–10: **"And lest I should be exalted above measure through the abundance of the revelations, there was given to me a thorn in the flesh, the messenger of Satan to buffet me, lest I should be exalted above measure. For this thing I besought the Lord thrice, that it might depart from me. And he said unto me, My grace is sufficient for thee: for my strength is made perfect in weakness. Most gladly therefore will I rather glory in my infirmities, that the power of Christ may rest upon me. Therefore I take pleasure in infirmities, in reproaches, in necessities, in persecutions, in distresses for Christ's sake: for when I am weak, then am I strong."**

I Timothy 5:23: **"Drink no longer water, but use a little wine for thy stomach's sake and thine often infirmities."**

II Timothy 4:20: **"Erastus abode at Corinth: but Trophimus have I left at Miletum sick."**

There was a time when Paul could send out handkerchiefs or aprons and the recipients could be healed.

> Acts 19:11,12: **"And God wrought special miracles by the hands of Paul: So that from his body were brought unto the sick handkerchiefs or aprons, and the diseases departed from them, and the evil spirits went out of them."**

After explaining to the Corinthians that the gifts were temporary, Paul had this to say:

> I Corinthians 13:11–13: **"When I was a child, I spake as a child, I understood as a child, I thought as a child: but when I became a man, I put away childish things. For now we see through a glass, darkly; but then face to face: now I know in part; but then shall I know even as also I am known. And now abideth** (Gr, *meno:* remain) **faith, hope, charity,** (Gr, *agape:* love) **these three; but the greatest of these** *is* **charity."**

Today, there are entire denominations trying to bring back the gifts of the Spirit. These are, for the most part, sincere brothers and sisters in Christ who need to ask themselves some sobering questions: If the Holy Spirit is not behind these gifts today, just who or what is behind their manifestation? Do you think it would be beneath the evil one to try to counterfeit these gifts to confuse the church today? Would it be more profitable to concentrate all efforts on those gifts that abideth (remain) in the power of the Holy Spirit, namely faith, hope, and love? In the former kingdom program Peter reported that believers received the gift of the Holy Spirit after they repented and were water baptized.

> Acts 2:38: **"Then Peter said unto them, Repent, and be baptized every one of you in the name of Jesus Christ for the remission of sins, and ye shall receive the gift of the Holy Ghost."**

In the present *mystery* program, Paul reports that we are indwelt by the Holy Spirit the moment we believe, and are baptized into (identified with) the body of Christ by the Spirit.

> I Corinthians 12:13: **"For by one Spirit are we all baptized into one body, whether** *we be* **Jews or Gentiles, whether** *we be* **bond or free; and have been all made to drink into one Spirit."**

> Romans 8:11: **"But if the Spirit of him that raised up Jesus from the dead dwell in you, he that raised up Christ from the dead shall also quicken your mortal bodies by his Spirit that dwelleth in you."**

> I Corinthians 3:16: **"Know ye not that ye are the temple of God, and** *that* **the Spirit of God dwelleth in you?"**

> II Timothy 1:14: **"That good thing which was committed unto thee keep by the Holy Ghost which dwelleth in us."**

Today, we have corporate ministry gifts for the body of Christ and personal ministry gifts for the members of that body.

> Ephesians 4:11,12: **"And he gave some, apostles; and some, prophets; and some, evangelists; and some, pastors and teachers; For the perfecting of the saints, for the work of the ministry, for the edifying of the body of Christ."**

It should be noted that there are no more apostles or prophets, now that the word of God is complete.

> Romans 12:6–8: **"Having then gifts differing according to the grace that is given to us, whether**

> prophecy, *let us prophesy* according to the pro-
> portion of faith; Or ministry, *let us wait* on *our*
> ministering: or he that teacheth, on teaching; Or
> he that exhorteth, on exhortation: he that giveth,
> *let him do it* with simplicity; he that ruleth, with
> diligence; he that sheweth mercy, with cheerful-
> ness."

It should be noted that the gift of prophesying is gone
from the scene, now that the word of God is complete.

PART 3

A TRIP THROUGH THE BIBLE

The Bible is inspired Holy Scripture authored by God through the Holy Spirit and reveals the various programs He has used in dealing with His creation. A fundamental premise is that the Bible can be understood, since God is not the author of confusion.

> I Corinthians 14:33: **"For God is not *the author* of confusion, but of peace, as in all churches of the saints."**

Creation
>4,000 B.C.

We find that in the beginning God created two distinctive parts, the heaven and the earth.

> Genesis 1:1: **"In the beginning God created the heaven and the earth."**

Man's Fall
4,000 B.C.

The creation of the earth included all life on the earth. Man and woman were created in a sinless state but at the first temptation, provided by the serpent, they sinned. This caused a change in God's program for them. He promised a **"Seed"** that would bruise the serpent's head, which we now know was Christ when He made the full payment for the sins of mankind with His death on the cross.

> **Genesis 3:14,15: "And the LORD God said unto the serpent, Because thou hast done this, thou *art* cursed above all cattle, and above every beast of the field; upon thy belly shalt thou go, and dust shalt thou eat all the days of thy life: And I will put enmity between thee and the woman, and between thy seed and her seed; it shall bruise thy head, and thou shalt bruise his heel."**

In the meantime God shed blood to cover the initial sin of Adam and Eve until the fulfillment of the promise of the "Seed."

> **Genesis 3:21: "Unto Adam also and to his wife did the LORD God make coats of skins, and clothed them."**

Flood Judgment
2,350 B.C.

As time went on the earth became populated, sinfulness increased, and finally God judged mankind and destroyed all life on the earth by means of a universal flood, except for Noah, his wife, his three sons, their three wives, and at least two of every form of animal life. After the flood God promised Noah that He would never again allow a flood to destroy all life on the earth. He placed a rainbow in the clouds as a sign of this promise and instructed Noah to replenish the earth.

> **Genesis 9:1: "And God blessed Noah and his sons, and said unto them, Be fruitful, and multiply, and replenish the earth."**

Babel Judgment
2,200 B.C.

However, as the earth was being repopulated, sinfulness once again increased, and mankind began to congregate in one area. Because of this disobedience God judged mankind and this time He scattered them over the earth by confusing their language.

> Genesis 11:1–9: **"And the whole earth was of one language, and of one speech. And it came to pass, as they journeyed from the east, that they found a plain in the land of Shinar; and they dwelt there. And they said one to another, Go to, let us make brick, and burn them thoroughly. And they had brick for stone, and slime had they for mortar. And they said, Go to, let us build us a city and a tower, whose top *may reach* unto heaven; and let us make us a name, lest we be scattered abroad upon the face of the whole earth. And the LORD came down to see the city and the tower, which the children of men builded. And the LORD said, Behold, the people *is* one, and they have all one language; and this they begin to do: and now nothing will be restrained from them, which they have imagined to do. Go to, let us go down, and there confound their language, that they may not understand one another's speech. So the LORD scattered them abroad from thence upon the face of all the earth: and they left off to build the city. Therefore is the name of it called Babel; because the LORD did there confound the language of all the earth: and from thence did the LORD scatter them abroad upon the face of all the earth."**

At this point God essentially concluded His dealings with mankind and men and women were known as **"nations," "heathen," "Gentiles,"** or **"Uncircumcision."**

> Deuteronomy 4:27: **"And the LORD shall scatter you among the nations, and ye shall be left few in number among the heathen, whither the LORD shall lead you."**

> Galatians 3:8: **"And the scripture, foreseeing that God would justify the heathen through faith, preached before the gospel unto Abraham,** *saying,* **In thee shall all nations be blessed."**

> Ephesians 2:11,12: **"Wherefore remember, that ye** *being* **in time past Gentiles in the flesh, who are called Uncircumcision by that which is called the Circumcision in the flesh made by hands; That at that time ye were without Christ, being aliens from the commonwealth of Israel, and strangers from the covenants of promise, having no hope, and without God in the world."**

Abraham, Isaac, and Jacob
1,930 B.C.

Next, God chose a man named Abram to begin a people He could have dealings with and also a people that could be a channel for the promised **"Seed."**

> Genesis 12:1–3: **"Now the LORD had said unto Abram, Get thee out of thy country, and from thy kindred, and from thy father's house, unto a land that I will shew thee: And I will make of thee a great nation, and I will bless thee, and make thy name great; and thou shalt be a blessing: And I will bless them that bless thee, and curse him that curseth thee: and in thee shall all families of the earth be blessed."**

Abram's name was later changed to Abraham and he became the father of the nation Israel. It is through Israel that God then channeled His dealings and planned to ultimately resume His dealings with the Gentiles as well.

Moses and the Law
1,500 B.C.

As the nation Israel grew, God gave them the Law through Moses, which consisted of more than 600 commandments, regulations, and ordinances.

Entering the Promised Land
1,460 B.C.

As the nation Israel began to take possession of the land promised to Abraham, they were under the leadership of Moses, Joshua, and the judges.

God the Father Rejected
1,125 B.C.

During the time of Samuel, who was to be the last judge, the Israelites rejected God the Father by demanding a king to judge them instead of having God reign over them.

> I Samuel 8:4–7: **"Then all the elders of Israel gathered themselves together, and came to Samuel unto Ramah, And said unto him, Behold, thou art old, and thy sons walk not in thy ways: now make us a king to judge us like all the nations. But the thing displeased Samuel, when they said, Give us a king to judge us. And Samuel prayed unto the LORD. And the LORD said unto Samuel, Hearken unto the voice of the people in all that they say unto thee: for they have not rejected thee, but they have rejected me, that I should not reign over them."**

As a result of this sin, the nation Israel never fully held possession of the Promised Land, even to this present day. Through the ministry of the prophets, God prophesied that He would send the Messiah to redeem Israel from her sin. This Messiah, born of the virgin Mary, was the Son of God in the person of Jesus Christ. God also promised Israel that He would establish an earthly kingdom where Jesus Christ Himself would reign as King, on the throne of David, and a tremendous time of peace and prosperity would result.

> Isaiah 9:6,7: **"For unto us a child is born, unto us a son is given: and the government shall be upon his shoulder: and his name shall be called Wonderful, Counsellor, The mighty God, The everlasting Father, The Prince of Peace. Of the increase of *his* government and peace *there shall be* no end, upon the throne of David, and upon his kingdom, to order it, and to establish it with judgment and with justice from henceforth even for ever. The zeal of the LORD of hosts will perform this."**

Jesus' Earthly Ministry
Circa 30 A.D.[5]

During the three-year earthly ministry of the Messiah, He preached repentance, that the kingdom of (from)[6] heaven was at hand, and this message was given to the Twelve Apostles to preach as well.

> Matthew 4:17: **"From that time Jesus began to preach, and to say, Repent: for the kingdom of heaven is at hand."**

> Matthew 10:5–7: **"These twelve Jesus sent forth, and commanded them, saying, Go not into the way of the Gentiles, and into *any* city of the**

---

[5]We know that the Lord's earthly ministry began when He was about thirty and our dating is off by perhaps four years. Luke 3:23: **"And Jesus himself began to be about thirty years of age,"**

[6]Kingdom *of* heaven is taken to mean coming *from* heaven (to earth).

Samaritans enter ye not: but go rather to the lost sheep of the house of Israel. And as ye go, preach, saying, The kingdom of heaven is at hand."

God the Son Rejected
33 A.D.

The nation Israel, for the most part, rejected her Messiah along with His message of forgiveness for their sins and His preaching of the coming prophesied kingdom. This rejection took the form of unbelief and demanding His crucifixion.

Matthew 27:22–25: **"Pilate saith unto them, What shall I do then with Jesus which is called Christ? *They* all say unto him, Let him be crucified. And the governor said, Why, what evil hath he done? But they cried out the more, saying, Let him be crucified. When Pilate saw that he could prevail nothing, but *that* rather a tumult was made, he took water, and washed *his* hands before the multitude, saying, I am innocent of the blood of this just person: see ye *to it.* Then answered all the people, and said, His blood *be* on us, and on our children."**

John 1:11: **"He came unto his own, and his own received him not."**

Israel's Commission
33 A.D.

Jesus Christ rose from the grave on the third day and instructed His disciples again to preach the gospel of the kingdom with water baptism for the remission of sins.

Matthew 28:19,20: **"Go ye therefore, and teach all nations, baptizing them in the name of the**

Father, and of the Son, and of the Holy Ghost: Teaching them to observe all things whatsoever I have commanded you: and, lo, I am with you alway, *even* unto the end of the world. Amen."

Mark 16:15–18: "And he said unto them, Go ye into all the world, and preach the gospel to every creature. He that believeth and is baptized shall be saved; but he that believeth not shall be damned. And these signs shall follow them that believe; In my name shall they cast out devils; they shall speak with new tongues; They shall take up serpents; and if they drink any deadly thing, it shall not hurt them; they shall lay hands on the sick, and they shall recover."

They were to begin with the nation Israel in Jerusalem and if Israel responded this time, they were to proceed with the same gospel in all Judaea, and in Samaria, and unto the uttermost part of the earth. The Lord then ascended to heaven after promising to send the Holy Spirit to empower them in this commission, usually known as the *Great Commission.*

Luke 24:46–49: "And said unto them, Thus it is written, and thus it behoved Christ to suffer, and to rise from the dead the third day: And that repentance and remission of sins should be preached in his name among all nations, beginning at Jerusalem. And ye are witnesses of these things. And, behold, I send the promise of my Father upon you: but tarry ye in the city of Jerusalem, until ye be endued with power from on high."

Acts 1:4–9: "And, being assembled together with *them,* commanded them that they should not depart from Jerusalem, but wait for the promise of the Father, which, *saith he,* ye have heard of me. For John truly baptized with water; but ye shall be baptized with the Holy Ghost not many days hence. When they therefore were come together, they asked of him, saying, Lord, wilt thou at this time restore again the kingdom to Israel? And he said unto them, It is not for you to know the times or the seasons, which the Father hath put in his own power. But ye shall receive power, after that the Holy Ghost is come upon you: and ye shall be witnesses unto me both in Jerusalem, and in all Judaea, and in Samaria, and unto the uttermost part of the earth. And when he had spoken these things, while they beheld, he was taken up; and a cloud received him out of their sight."

The water ceremony of baptism was part of the fulfillment of God's conditional promise, through Moses, that the Israelites would become a **"kingdom of priests"** in the coming earthly kingdom if they would obey His voice and keep His covenant. This washing or baptism was done in conjunction with the blood sacrifice in preparation for the priesthood.

Exodus 19:5,6: **"Now therefore, if ye will obey my voice indeed, and keep my covenant, then ye shall be a peculiar treasure unto me above all people: for all the earth *is* mine: And ye shall be unto me a kingdom of priests, and an holy nation. These *are* the words which thou shalt speak unto the children of Israel."**

Revelation 20:6: **"Blessed and holy *is* he that hath part in the first resurrection: on such the second death hath no power, but they shall be priests of God and of Christ, and shall reign with him a thousand years."**

Exodus 29:1–4: **"And this *is* the thing that thou shalt do unto them to hallow them, to minister unto me in the priest's office: Take one young bullock, and two rams without blemish, And unleavened bread, and cakes unleavened tempered with oil, and wafers unleavened anointed with oil:** *of* **wheaten flour shalt thou make them. And thou shalt put them into one basket, and bring them in the basket, with the bullock and the two rams. And Aaron and his sons thou shalt bring unto the door of the tabernacle of the congregation, and shalt wash them with water."**

Exodus 29:10,11: **"And thou shalt cause a bullock to be brought before the tabernacle of the congregation: and Aaron and his sons shall put their hands upon the head of the bullock. And thou shalt kill the bullock before the LORD,** *by* **the door of the tabernacle of the congregation."**

Ezekiel 36:25: **"Then will I sprinkle clean water upon you, and ye shall be clean: from all your filthiness, and from all your idols, will I cleanse you."**

With the preaching of the **"kingdom of** (from) **heaven at hand,"** the Israelites were now ready to become that **"kingdom of priests"** if they would believe and submit to water baptism.

Matthew 3:1–6: **"In those days came John the Baptist, preaching in the wilderness of Judaea, And saying, Repent ye: for the kingdom of heaven is at hand. For this is he that was spoken of by the prophet Esaias, saying, The voice of one crying in the wilderness, Prepare ye the way of the Lord, make his paths straight. And the same John had his raiment of camel's hair, and a** leathern girdle about his loins; and his meat was locusts and wild honey. Then went out to him Jerusalem, and all Judaea, and all the region round about Jordan, And were baptized of him in Jordan, confessing their sins."

Matthew 4:17: "From that time Jesus began to preach, and to say, Repent: for the kingdom of heaven is at hand."

Coming of the Holy Spirit
33 A.D.

As you begin reading the book of Acts, you find the apostles being filled with the Holy Spirit on the day of Pentecost and Peter preaching the gospel of the kingdom as the Lord had instructed. The people of the nation Israel now need not only to repent of their broken covenant relationship with God but also to repent of the sin of murder in crucifying their Messiah.

Acts 2:22,23: "Ye men of Israel, hear these words; Jesus of Nazareth, a man approved of God among you by miracles and wonders and signs, which God did by him in the midst of you, as ye yourselves also know: Him, being delivered by the determinate counsel and foreknowledge of God, ye have taken, and by wicked hands have crucified and slain."

Acts 2:36–38: "Therefore let all the house of Israel know assuredly, that God hath made that same Jesus, whom ye have crucified, both Lord and Christ. Now when they heard *this,* they were pricked in their heart, and said unto Peter and to the rest of the apostles, Men *and* brethren, what shall we do? Then Peter said unto them, repent, and be baptized every one of you in the name

of Jesus Christ for the remission of sins, and ye shall receive the gift of the Holy Ghost."

The Bible records that about three thousand souls were added to the Jewish Church as a result of Peter's Pentecostal address. In his next address/sermon the charge of murder was lessened by acknowledging their ignorance, and the promised kingdom was finally offered. This agrees with our Lord's prayer on the cross, Luke 23:34: **" . . . Father, forgive them; for they know not what they do."**

Acts 3:13–21: **"The God of Abraham, and of Isaac, and of Jacob, the God of our fathers, hath glorified his Son Jesus; whom ye delivered up, and denied him in the presence of Pilate, when he was determined to let *him* go. But ye denied the Holy One and the Just, and desired a murderer to be granted unto you; And killed the Prince of life, whom God hath raised from the dead; whereof we are witnesses. And his name through faith in his name hath made this man strong, whom ye see and know: yea, the faith which is by him hath given him this perfect soundness in the presence of you all. And now, brethren, I wot that through ignorance ye did *it,* as *did* also your rulers. But those things, which God before had shewed by the mouth of all his prophets, that Christ should suffer, he hath so fulfilled. Repent ye therefore, and be converted, that your sins may be blotted out, when the times of refreshing shall come from the presence of the Lord; And he shall send Jesus Christ, which before was preached unto you: Whom the heaven must receive until the times of restitution of all things, which God hath spoken by the mouth of all his holy prophets since the world began."**

Despite the fact that many had responded earlier, the majority in the nation Israel along with her leaders rejected this offer.

> Luke 7:29,30: **"And all the people that heard** *him,* **and the publicans, justified God, being baptized with the baptism of John. But the Pharisees and lawyers rejected the counsel of God against themselves, being not baptized of him."**

If this wasn't enough Israel's leaders also began persecuting the apostles who were preaching the gospel of the kingdom.

> Acts 4:1–3: **"And as they spake unto the people, the priests, and the captain of the temple, and the Sadducees, came upon them, Being grieved that they taught the people, and preached through Jesus the resurrection from the dead. And they laid hands on them, and put** *them* **in hold unto the next day: for it was now eventide."**

According to the following parable in Luke, Israel was expected to produce fruit during the three-year ministry of Christ. When this didn't happen the extra year was granted, during which insufficient fruit was produced and the persecution of the few continued.

> Luke 13:6–9: **"He spake also this parable; A certain** *man* **had a fig tree planted in his vineyard; and he came and sought fruit thereon, and found none. Then said he unto the dresser of his vineyard, Behold, these three years I come seeking fruit on this fig tree, and find none: cut it down; why cumbereth it the ground? And he answering said unto him, Lord, let it alone this year also, till I shall dig about it, and dung** *it:*

And if it bear fruit, *well:* and if not, *then* after that thou shalt cut it down."

God the Holy Spirit Rejected
34 A.D.

Despite much persecution God allowed His program to continue unchanged for the extra year, until Stephen was stoned to death by the Jewish leaders. It was at this time that the nation Israel resisted, or blasphemed, the third person of the Godhead, the Holy Spirit.

Acts 7:51–60: **"Ye stiffnecked and uncircumcised in heart and ears, ye do always resist the Holy Ghost: as your fathers *did,* so *do* ye. Which of the prophets have not your fathers persecuted? and they have slain them which shewed before of the coming of the Just One; of whom ye have been now the betrayers and murderers: Who have received the law by the disposition of angels, and have not kept *it.* When they heard these things, they were cut to the heart, and they gnashed on him with *their* teeth. But he, being full of the Holy Ghost, looked up stedfastly into heaven, and saw the glory of God, and Jesus standing on the right hand of God, And said, Behold, I see the heavens opened, and the Son of man standing on the right hand of God. Then they cried out with a loud voice, and stopped their ears, and ran upon him with one accord, And cast *him* out of the city, and stoned *him:* and the witnesses laid down their clothes at a young man's feet, whose name was Saul. And they stoned Stephen, calling upon *God,* and saying, Lord Jesus, receive my spirit. And he kneeled down, and cried with a loud voice, Lord, lay not this sin to their charge. And when he had said this, he fell asleep."**

This was the third and final chance for Israel. First, they had rejected God the Father by demanding a king under Samuel. Second, they had rejected God the Son at the cross. Now, their rejection of God the Holy Spirit through Stephen resulted in their committing the unpardonable sin about which they had been warned.

> Matthew 12:31,32: **"Wherefore I say unto you, All manner of sin and blasphemy shall be forgiven unto men: but the blasphemy** *against* **the** *Holy* **Ghost shall not be forgiven unto men. And whosoever speaketh a word against the Son of man, it shall be forgiven him: but whosoever speaketh against the Holy Ghost, it shall not be forgiven him, neither in this world, neither in the** *world* **to come."**

After the stoning of Stephen, the unrepentant Jews began to unrelentingly persecute the Jewish church. This **"great persecution"** began in Jerusalem and scattered that church abroad. There are two noteworthy aspects of this scattering of the Jewish church: first, the apostles stayed at Jerusalem in obedience to their commission from the Lord; and second, the scattered Jewish church preached the word to the Jews only (the Gentiles will be dealt with shortly) in obedience to the commission from the Lord.

> Acts 8:1–4: **"And Saul was consenting unto his death. And at that time there was a great persecution against the church which was at Jerusalem; and they were all scattered abroad throughout the regions of Judaea and Samaria, except the apostles. And devout men carried Stephen** *to his burial,* **and made great lamentation over him. As for Saul, he made havock of the church, entering into every house, and haling men and women committed** *them* **to prison. Therefore they that**

were scattered abroad went every where preaching the word."

Acts 11:19: **"Now they which were scattered abroad upon the persecution that arose about Stephen travelled as far as Phenice, and Cyprus, and Antioch, preaching the word to none but unto the Jews only."**

Israel's Prophecy Interrupted
(Saul of Tarsus Converted)
34 A.D.

It was at this point that God began to change the program of His dealings with the nation Israel. First, Jesus Christ Himself struck down Saul, also known as Paul, on his way to Damascus. Then He saved Paul, commissioned him an apostle, and through a series of revelations communicated a new program whereby salvation would be offered directly to the Gentiles in spite of Israel's rejection of her Messiah and subsequent fall. At this time God temporarily set aside the kingdom program with the Jews and began a new program, called *the mystery,* to both Jews and Gentiles. The term *mystery* means that you can't find this program forecast in the prophetic Scriptures, it was **"hid in God."**

II Corinthians 12:1: **"It is not expedient for me doubtless to glory. I will come to visions and revelations of the Lord."**

Romans 11:11: **"I say then, Have they stumbled that they should fall? God forbid: but *rather* through their fall salvation *is come* unto the Gentiles, for to provoke them to jealousy."**

Romans 11:25,32: **"For I would not, brethren, that ye should be ignorant of this mystery, lest ye should be wise in your own conceits; that blind-**

ness in part is happened to Israel, until the fulness of the Gentiles be come in. For God hath
concluded them all in unbelief, that he might
have mercy upon all."

Ephesians 3:1–9: "For this cause I Paul, the prisoner of Jesus Christ for you Gentiles, If ye have
heard of the dispensation of the grace of God
which is given me to you-ward: How that by revelation he made known unto me the mystery; (as
I wrote afore in few words, Whereby, when ye
read, ye may understand my knowledge in the
mystery of Christ) Which in other ages was not
made known unto the sons of men, as it is now
revealed unto his holy apostles and prophets by
the Spirit; That the Gentiles should be fellow-
heirs, and of the same body, and partakers of
his promise in Christ by the gospel: Whereof
I was made a minister, according to the gift of
the grace of God given unto me by the effectual
working of his power. Unto me, who am less than
the least of all saints, is this grace given, that I
should preach among the Gentiles the unsearchable riches of Christ; And to make all *men* see
what *is* the fellowship of the mystery, which from
the beginning of the world hath been <u>hid in God</u>,
who created all things by Jesus Christ."

The Church the Body of Christ
Present

The terms of the new program resulted in Paul preaching
a new **"gospel of the grace of God,"** whereby individuals
can be saved by truly believing in the death, burial and
resurrection of Christ and that He died for their sins.
The difference in this gospel is that Christ's blood
and His blood alone is sufficient payment for all past,

present, and future sins of those who believe this gospel of God's grace.

> Acts 20:21,24: **"Testifying both to the Jews, and also to the Greeks, repentance toward God, and faith toward our Lord Jesus Christ. But none of these things move me, neither count I my life dear unto myself, so that I might finish my course with joy, and the ministry, which I have received of the Lord Jesus, to testify the <u>gospel of the grace of God.</u>"**

> I Corinthians 15:1–4: **"Moreover, brethren, I declare unto you the <u>gospel</u> which I preached unto you, which also ye have received, and wherein ye stand; By which also ye are saved, if ye keep in memory what I preached unto you, unless ye have believed in vain. For I delivered unto you first of all that which I also received, how that Christ died for our sins according to the scriptures; And that he was buried, and that he rose again the third day according to the scriptures."**

> Galatians 1:8: **"But though we, or an angel from heaven, preach any other gospel unto you than that which we have preached unto you, let him be accursed."**

> Ephesians 2:8,9: **"For by grace are ye saved through faith; and that not of yourselves:** *it is* **the gift of God: Not of works, lest any man should boast."**

> Colossians 2:13: **"And you, being dead in your sins and the uncircumcision of your flesh, hath he quickened together with him, having forgiven you all trespasses."**

Earlier, we identified the *Great Commission* as it related to the preaching of the *gospel of the kingdom.* Now, let's take a look at the *current commission* as it relates to the preaching of the *gospel of the grace of God.* There are two aspects to the current commission. First, God has reconciled us to Himself by Jesus Christ and has given us the ministry of reconciliation as ambassadors for Christ. Second, according to the example of the Apostle Paul, we preach the unsearchable riches of Christ and help all see the fellowship of the *mystery.* The word fellowship (Gr, *koinonia:* participation, communion) suggests: the loving[7] participation and communion among members of the body of Christ in the *mystery.*

II Corinthians 5:17–21: **"Therefore if any man** *be* **in Christ,** *he is* **a new creature: old things are passed away; behold, all things are become new. And all things** *are* **of God, who hath reconciled us to himself by Jesus Christ, and hath given to us the ministry of reconciliation; To wit, that God was in Christ, reconciling the world unto himself, not imputing their trespasses unto them; and hath committed unto us the word of reconciliation. Now then we are ambassadors for Christ, as though God did beseech** *you* **by us: we pray** *you* **in Christ's stead, be ye reconciled to God. For he hath made him** *to be* **sin for us, who knew no sin; that we might be made the righteousness of God in him."**

Ephesians 3:8–12: **"Unto me, who am less than the least of all saints, is this grace given, that I should preach among the Gentiles the unsearchable riches of Christ; And to make all** *men* **see what is the fellowship of the mystery, which from the beginning of the world hath been hid in God, who created all things by Jesus Christ: To the in-**

---

[7]The dimension of *love* (it's the pinnacle) will be dealt with, in detail, in Book Two.

tent that now unto the principalities and powers in heavenly *places* might be known by the church the manifold wisdom of God, According to the eternal purpose which he purposed in Christ Jesus our Lord: In whom we have boldness and access with confidence by the faith of him."

The complete changeover from the *prophetic* program to the *mystery* program took about thirty years as the Apostle Paul was receiving revelations from the ascended Lord Jesus Christ. Just as the Jews failed to see that their program with God had changed then, today, many Christians are combining the previous program with the current one called the *mystery*. It is no wonder that there are over 400 denominations today that differ in relation to what parts of the old program are combined with the new *mystery* program. This new *mystery* program with the gospel of the grace of God and the church, which is His body, will continue **"until the fulness of the Gentiles [full number of the Gentiles][8] be come in."** (More on this in Part 4)

II Corinthians 12:1: **"It is not expedient for me doubtless to glory. I will come to visions and revelations of the Lord."**

Acts 28:27,28: **"For the heart of this people is waxed gross, and their ears are dull of hearing, and their eyes have they closed; lest they should see with *their* eyes, and hear with *their* ears, and understand with *their* heart, and should be converted, and I should heal them. Be it known therefore unto you, that the salvation of God is sent unto the Gentiles, and *that* they will hear it."**

Romans 11:25: **"For I would not, brethren, that ye should be ignorant of this mystery, lest ye should**

---

[8]Gr, *pleroma:* completion

be wise in your own conceits; that blindness in part is happened to Israel, until the fulness of the Gentiles be come in."

Romans 16:25: "Now to him that is of power to stablish you according to my gospel, and the preaching of Jesus Christ, according to the revelation of the mystery, which was kept secret since the world began,"

Ephesians 1:22,23: "And hath put all *things* under his feet, and gave him *to be* the head over all *things* to the church, Which is his body, the fulness of him that filleth all in all."

I Thessalonians 4:13–18: "But I would not have you to be ignorant, brethren, concerning them which are asleep, that ye sorrow not, even as others which have no hope. For if we believe that Jesus died and rose again, even so them also which sleep in Jesus will God bring with him. For this we say unto you by the word of the Lord, that we which are alive *and* remain unto the coming of the Lord shall not prevent them which are asleep. For the Lord himself shall descend from heaven with a shout, with the voice of the archangel, and with the trump of God: and the dead in Christ shall rise first: Then we which are alive *and* remain shall be caught up together with them in the clouds, to meet the Lord in the air: and so shall we ever be with the Lord. Wherefore comfort one another with these words."

I Corinthians 15:51,52: "Behold, I shew you a mystery; We shall not all sleep, but we shall all be changed, In a moment, in the twinkling of an eye, at the last trump: for the trumpet shall

sound, and the dead shall be raised incorrupt-
ible, and we shall be changed."

Israel's Prophecy Resumed
Future

Once **"the fulness of the Gentiles be come in,"** the Lord
will take the church, His body, to heaven, and God's
prophetic program on the earth with Israel will resume.
It will begin with the tribulation period, lasting seven
years, and will include Christ's second coming to earth to
establish the promised earthly kingdom. It is then that He
will reign as King on David's throne. He will resurrect the
kingdom saints of all ages and the Twelve Apostles will
sit on thrones judging the twelve tribes of Israel.

> Luke 1:32,33: **"He shall be great, and shall be
> called the Son of the Highest: and the Lord God
> shall give unto him the throne of his father David:
> And he shall reign over the house of Jacob for
> ever; and of his kingdom there shall be no end."**

> Matthew 19:28: **"And Jesus said unto them, Verily
> I say unto you, That ye which have followed me,
> in the regeneration when the Son of man shall
> sit in the throne of his glory, ye also shall sit
> upon twelve thrones, judging the twelve tribes
> of Israel."**

> Luke 22:30: **"That ye may eat and drink at my
> table in my kingdom, and sit on thrones judging
> the twelve tribes of Israel."**

> Acts 2:29,30: **"Men *and* brethren, let me freely
> speak unto you of the patriarch David, that he
> is both dead and buried, and his sepulchre is
> with us unto this day. Therefore being a proph-
> et, and knowing that God had sworn with an
> oath to him, that of the fruit of his loins, ac-**

cording to the flesh, he would raise up Christ
to sit on his throne."

Israel's Earthly Kingdom
Future

The first phase of this kingdom we now know will last
1,000 years, during which time Satan will be bound and
cast into the bottomless pit. At the end of 1,000 years,
Satan will be **"loosed out of his prison,"** and he will **"go
out to deceive the nations."**

Revelation 20:1–8: **"And I saw an angel come
down from heaven, having the key of the bottomless pit and a great chain in his hand. And he
laid hold on the dragon, that old serpent, which
is the Devil, and Satan, and bound him a thousand years, And cast him into the bottomless
pit, and shut him up, and set a seal upon him,
that he should deceive the nations no more, till
the thousand years should be fulfilled: and after
that he must be loosed a little season. And I saw
thrones, and they sat upon them, and judgment
was given unto them: and *I saw* the souls of them
that were beheaded for the witness of Jesus, and
for the word of God, and which had not worshipped the beast, neither his image, neither
had received *his* mark upon their foreheads, or
in their hands; and they lived and reigned with
Christ a thousand years. But the rest of the dead
lived not again until the thousand years were finished. This *is* the first resurrection. Blessed and
holy *is* he that hath part in the first resurrection:
on such the second death hath no power, but
they shall be priests of God and of Christ, and
shall reign with him a thousand years. And when
the thousand years are expired, Satan shall be
loosed out of his prison, And shall go out to de-**

ceive the nations which are in the four quarters of the earth, Gog and Magog, to gather them together to battle: the number of whom *is* as the sand of the sea."

Final Judgment
Future

This time God will quickly end the final outbreak of sin on the earth. He will then resurrect and judge the unsaved of all ages at the **"great white throne,"** and usher in the eternal state where the saved of all programs will occupy **"a new heaven and a new earth,"** and the unsaved of all programs will be **"cast into the lake of fire."** From then on sin will be no more and the saved will spend eternity with God the Father, the Lord Jesus Christ, and the Holy Spirit in a sinless state as it was in the beginning, when God created the heaven and the earth.

Revelation 20:9–15: **"And they went up on the breadth of the earth, and compassed the camp of the saints about, and the beloved city: and fire came down from God out of heaven, and devoured them. And the devil that deceived them was cast into the lake of fire and brimstone, where the beast and the false prophet *are,* and shall be tormented day and night for ever and ever. And I saw a great white throne, and him that sat on it, from whose face the earth and the heaven fled away; and there was found no place for them. And I saw the dead, small and great, stand before God; and the books were opened: and another book was opened, which is *the book* of life: and the dead were judged out of those things which were written in the books, according to their works. And the sea gave up the dead which were in it; and death and hell delivered up the dead which were in them: and** they were judged every man according to their works. And death and hell were cast into the lake of fire. This is the second death. And whosoever was not found written in the book of life was cast into the lake of fire."

New Heaven and New Earth
Future

Revelation 21:1,2: "**And I saw a new heaven and a new earth: for the first heaven and the first earth were passed away; and there was no more sea. And I John saw the holy city, new Jerusalem, coming down from God out of heaven, prepared as a bride adorned for her husband.**"

Consummation

Ephesians 1:10: "**That in the dispensation of the fulness of times he might gather together in one all things in Christ, both which are in heaven, and which are on earth; *even* in him.**"

I Corinthians 15:24–28: "**Then *cometh* the end, when he shall have delivered up the kingdom to God, even the Father; when he shall have put down all rule and all authority and power. For he must reign, till he hath put all enemies under his feet. The last enemy *that* shall be destroyed *is* death. For he hath put all things under his feet. But when he saith all things are put under *him, it is* manifest that he is excepted, which did put all things under him. And when all things shall be subdued unto him, then shall the Son also himself be subject unto him that put all things under him, that God may be all in all.**"

PART 4

A BIBLICAL LOOK AT END TIMES

With a mid-Acts dispensational view on the subject of End Times, one finds that the prophetic program was put on temporary hold. This was due to the majority of Israel rejecting her Messiah during the ministry of the twelve as well as their resisting the Holy Spirit at the stoning of Stephen. God responded in matchless grace with the raising up of the Apostle Paul. It was unto him that the risen, ascended, and glorified Lord Jesus Christ communicated through a series of direct, heavenly revelations, the new program of God's grace known as the *mystery*. It's called the *mystery* because you can't find it forecast in the prophetic Scriptures. The only indirect hint we have as to how long this new program will last is in Romans 11:25,26. Here, we learn that blindness in part has happened to Israel until the fulness of the Gentiles be come in and then all Israel shall be saved. Blindness in part (Gr, *meros:* piece, portion) means that it affected a piece or portion of Israel and we know from the context (i.e., "until") that it will be temporary.

> Romans 11:25,26: **"For I would not, brethren, that ye should be ignorant of this mystery, lest ye should be wise in your own conceits; that blindness in part is happened to Israel, until the fulness of the Gentiles be come in. And so all**

> **Israel shall be saved: as it is written, There shall come out of Sion the Deliverer, and shall turn away ungodliness from Jacob."**

The condition where God will remove the blindness in part is that **"the fulness (Gr,** *pleroma:* completion) **of the Gentiles be come in."** *Pleroma* suggests that as Gentiles are being added to the body of Christ, there is a point in which the *completion* of this process will arrive. I take this to mean the full complement, or number of Gentiles becoming saved. Since no one but God knows how many more it will take or how long it will take, the *rapture* could happen at any moment.[9] Once this fulness is achieved and the *rapture* occurs, God will work to save all Israel by first of all removing the *blindness.* We know that this will involve a time of tribulation, judgment, and preaching of the gospel of the kingdom. This time, without the *blindness,* Israel will be taken to a point of belief and trust. This time is called the *day of the Lord.* (Note the prophecy in Joel and its partial fulfillment in Acts.)

> Joel 2:28–32: **"And it shall come to pass afterward,** *that* **I will pour out my spirit upon all flesh; and your sons and your daughters shall prophesy, your old men shall dream dreams, your young men shall see visions: And also upon the servants and upon the handmaids in those days will I pour out my spirit. And I will shew wonders in the heavens and in the earth, blood, and fire, and pillars of smoke. The sun shall be turned into darkness, and the moon into blood, before the great and the terrible day of the LORD come. And it shall come to pass,** *that* **whosoever shall call on the name of the LORD shall be delivered: for in mount Zion and in Jerusalem shall be deliverance, as the LORD hath said, and in the remnant whom the LORD shall call."**

---

[9] Isn't it sobering to think that the *rapture* could happen as you are leading someone to Christ, the moment they believe, and isn't it also sobering to think that once the *rapture* occurs, you will lose the opportunity to talk to your friends and family about trusting Christ?

Acts 2:16–21: **"But this is that which was spoken by the prophet Joel; And it shall come to pass in the last days, saith God, I will pour out of my Spirit upon all flesh: and your sons and your daughters shall prophesy, and your young men shall see visions, and your old men shall dream dreams: And on my servants and on my handmaidens I will pour out in those days of my Spirit; and they shall prophesy: And I will shew wonders in heaven above, and signs in the earth beneath; blood, and fire, and vapour of smoke: The sun shall be turned into darkness, and the moon into blood, before that great and notable <u>day of the Lord</u> come: And it shall come to pass,** *that* **whosoever shall call on the name of the Lord shall be saved."**

I Thessalonians 5:2: **"For yourselves know perfectly that the <u>day of the Lord</u> so cometh as a thief in the night."**

How do we know that once the *blindness* is removed from Israel, she will respond to the gospel of the kingdom this time? Let's look to the Scriptures for our answer:

Zechariah 12:9,10: **"And it shall come to pass in that day,** *that* **I will seek to destroy all the nations that come against Jerusalem. And I will pour upon the house of David, and upon the inhabitants of Jerusalem, the spirit of grace and of supplications: and they shall look upon me whom they have pierced, and they shall mourn for him, as one mourneth for** *his* **only** *son,* **and shall be in bitterness for him, as one that is in bitterness for** *his* **firstborn."**

The prophetic clock will be restarting after the *rapture* of the body of Christ. The man of sin (the Anti-Christ, the beast) will be revealed and the day of the Lord will begin as foretold in the book of Revelation.

During Paul's ministry of approximately thirty years he had to constantly fight against false doctrine. One such false doctrine was that the day of the Lord had already come. In his second letter to the Thessalonians he addressed this issue:

> II Thessalonians 2:1–3: **"Now we beseech you, brethren, by the coming of our Lord Jesus Christ, and** *by* **our gathering together unto him. That ye be not soon shaken in mind, or be troubled, neither by spirit, nor by word, nor by letter as from us, as that the day of Christ is at hand. Let no man deceive you by any means: for** *that day shall not come,* **except there come a falling away first, and that man of sin be revealed, the son of perdition."**

In Paul's first letter to the Thessalonians, he described in detail the future **"gathering together unto Him"** (see I Thessalonians 4:13–18). The term we use today for this event is the *rapture*. Although the word *rapture* is not found in our English translations, there is a Greek word (*apostasia*)[10] in verse three above that has the idea. That word is translated **"a falling away"** and the Greek definite article (*the*) is supplied in the original and suggests *the* departure. I know a lady who grew up in Greece and although the Modern Greek is much changed from the Greek in our New Testaments, many of the words are still in usage today. I asked her about the Greek word *apostasia* and she told me how her father used it with her. He told her that if she found herself with others that were talking about things or doing things of which he didn't approve, she was to *apostasia*. At that point she tore a piece from a page of paper in front of her and tossed it

---

[10] This word appears to have a dual meaning, it's used one other time in Acts 21:21: "... **thou teachest all the Jews which are among the Gentiles to** *forsake* **Moses ...**" it carries the idea of *depart* (from Moses). Many translations also use *apostasy* or *rebellion* in II Thessalonians 2:3.

across the table. She was to *depart* from that group! With that in mind, let's paraphrase the three verses above from II Thessalonians 2:1–3:

We ask you, based of the fact that Jesus Christ is going to come and gather us unto him, not to be upset by false teachers that come and say that this day or the day of the Lord has already come. That day has not come yet and won't come until the rapture happens and that man of sin be revealed, the son of perdition.

In the next verses Paul says a few words about why the man of sin, the Anti-Christ, won't be revealed until after the *rapture*.

II Thessalonians 2:5–7: **"Remember ye not, that, when I was yet with you, I told you these things? And now ye know what withholdeth that he might be revealed in his time. For the mystery of iniquity doth already work: only he who now letteth *will let*, until he be taken out of the way."**

Many take these verses to mean that it is the Holy Spirit **"what withholdeth"** (Gr, *katecho:* to hold down) and is **"he who now letteth"** (Gr, *katecho:* to hold down). This may be true; however, we also know that the Holy Spirit indwells all believers today and that after the *rapture* the restraining influence of Spirit-filled Christians will be gone from the earth. The Holy Spirit, on the other hand, will still be on earth as Israel is being saved in the tribulation as we will see. If it is the Holy Spirit who is **"what withholdeth"** and is **"he who now letteth"** I believe He is doing it through the believers that live on the earth at this time.

After the *rapture* the next thing on the timetable will be the events as they unfold in the book of Revelation. Around a century ago Sir Robert Anderson made the observation that: "A thousand years *could* expire after the *rapture* before the events of Revelation start without violating a single line of Scripture." Most people think the events of Revelation will start immediately, but only God knows for sure. One thing *is* sure; it won't matter to us as Christians since we will not be here to wonder about it!

Let's preface the discussion of the events that will happen in the day of the Lord with a look at the tribulation period and how long it will last. In order to do this we will go to Daniel the prophet where we read:

> Daniel 9:24–26: **"Seventy weeks are determined upon thy people and upon thy holy city, to finish the transgression, and to make an end of sins, and to make reconciliation for iniquity, and to bring in everlasting righteousness, and to seal up the vision and prophecy, and to anoint the most Holy. Know therefore and understand,** *that* **from the going forth of the commandment to restore and to build Jerusalem unto the Messiah the Prince** *shall be* **seven weeks, and threescore and two weeks: the street shall be built again, and the wall, even in troublous times. And after threescore and two weeks shall Messiah be cut off, but not for himself: and the people of the prince that shall come shall destroy the city and the sanctuary; and the end thereof** *shall be* **with a flood, and unto the end of the war desolations are determined."**

These seventy weeks represent seventy weeks of years or 490 years. The use of a week to represent seven years is found elsewhere such as in Genesis 29:18,27,28:

> **"And Jacob loved Rachel; and said, I will serve thee seven years for Rachel thy younger daughter. Fulfil her week, and we will give thee**

> **this also for the service which thou shalt serve with me yet seven other years. And Jacob did so, and fulfilled her week: and he gave him Rachel his daughter to wife also."**

It would take another complete book to fully discuss the entire body of truth contained in the 70 weeks of year's prophecy; however, what you would find is that 483 of the 490 years, or 69 of the 70 weeks, were accomplished by the time of the stoning of Stephen. Therefore, the tribulation will last for seven years with the most severe portion being the last half of 42 months or 1,260 days. Without understanding the *mystery* and the resulting interruption of the prophetic program, it would be impossible to explain why the last seven years, or seventieth week, haven't yet happened. It is clear from the Acts record that the finishing of the 70 weeks or 490 years was to be a continuous process, Acts 2:16–21:

16 "But this is that which was spoken by the prophet Joel;
17 "And it shall come to pass in the last days, saith God, I will pour out of my Spirit upon all flesh: and your sons and your daughters shall prophesy, and your young men shall see visions, and your old men shall dream dreams:
18 "And on my servants and on my handmaidens I will pour out in those days of my Spirit; and they shall prophesy:

(By the grace of God this prophecy was interrupted by the *mystery*.)

19 "And I will shew wonders in heaven above, and signs in the earth beneath; blood, and fire, and vapour of smoke:

20 "The sun shall be turned into darkness, and the moon into blood, before that great and notable day of the Lord come:
21 "And it shall come to pass, *that* whosoever shall call on the name of the Lord shall be saved."

We know that the end can't come (i.e., the battle of Armageddon) until the gospel of the kingdom is preached in all the world and this will require Israel to be saved first before going to all nations. We find in Matthew 24:14: **"And this gospel of the kingdom shall be preached in all the world for a witness unto all nations; and then shall the end come."** We know that the apostles were told in Luke 24:47: **"And that repentance and remission of sins should be preached in his name among all nations, beginning at Jerusalem."** Also they were told in Acts 1:8: **"But ye shall receive power, after that the Holy Ghost is come upon you: and ye shall be witnesses unto me both in Jerusalem, and in all Judaea, and in Samaria, and unto the uttermost part of the earth."** Well, after the stoning of Stephen, a *great* persecution began against these efforts and to this day the gospel of the kingdom hasn't been **"preached in all the world for a witness unto all nations."** Stay tuned, however, and we will see how that will be accomplished in a miraculous way in the first half of the *tribulation.* As I did in the verses above, I have drawn a blue line in my Bible between verse 18 and 19 of Acts 2 and written: *By the grace of God this prophecy was interrupted by the mystery.*

Before we move on in our study, let's search the Scriptures as good Bereans[11] and verify that the gospel of the kingdom wasn't then and hasn't yet been preached in all the world.

Acts 8:1: **"And Saul was consenting unto his death. And at that time there was a great persecu-**

---

[11]Acts 17:11 "These [Bereans] were more noble than those in Thessalonica, in that they received the word with all readiness of mind, and searched the scriptures daily, whether those things were so."

tion against the church which was at Jerusalem; and they were all scattered abroad throughout the regions of Judaea and Samaria, <u>except the apostles.</u>"

Acts 11:19: **"Now they which were scattered abroad upon the persecution that arose about Stephen travelled as far as Phenice, and Cyprus, and Antioch, preaching the word to <u>none but unto the Jews only.</u>"**

I believe that the two verses above demonstrate that: 1) the apostles didn't venture on to the next step in the process that would take the gospel of the kingdom[12] to the world and there is no record that they ever did, and 2) the Jews who were dispersed in the great persecution preached the word to **"none but the Jews only."** So the gospel of the kingdom didn't travel to the world through them either. It's interesting that the Holy Spirit gave us these details, the meaning of which could easily be missed. Without these two details we would have to rely on historical evidence alone to determine whether or not the kingdom gospel was preached beyond Jerusalem.[13]

Try to imagine the chaos that would be present in the world if millions of Christians were to disappear in an instant. Certainly, there would be enormous problems to solve in governments, businesses, private sectors, as well as churches. Amid all this confusion how will God restart the prophetic clock with no Christians to preach the gospel of the kingdom? Well, God has never before been without a witness on earth and He won't this time either. In Revelation 11:3 John is inspired to write what I referred to earlier as *a miraculous way* that the gospel of the kingdom will be preached in the tribulation: **"And I will give *power* unto my two witnesses, and they shall prophesy a thousand two hundred *and* threescore days, clothed**

---

[12] The word *gospel* is best not used alone but along with *kingdom* or *grace of God* to show which gospel is being referred to, i.e., the gospel of the kingdom or the gospel of the grace of God.

[13] When Peter went to Cornelius in Acts 10 he was on a special mission, to Gentiles, and didn't go because Israel was converted and wasn't moving out based on the Great Commission.

in sackcloth." We know from the same passage that they are killed, then raised, and then, midway through the *tribulation,* they ascend to heaven. So, if they prophesied 1,260 days, that would place their arrival in Jerusalem at the beginning of the tribulation period. I believe that they will be preaching the gospel of the kingdom immediately after the *rapture* and the firstfruits of their ministry will be the 144,000 Jews from Revelation 7:4: **"And I heard the number of them which were sealed:** *and there were* **sealed an hundred** *and* **forty** *and* **four thousand of all the tribes of the children of Israel."**

Right on the heels of the 144,000 being sealed, seven churches will be established in Asia. It will be from this base that Israel will be saved and the gospel of the kingdom will be able to go around the world, to all nations, before the end can come. This will be possible notwithstanding the Anti-Christ running loose because he will make a covenant with Israel for one week (seven years). During the first half of this covenant the gospel will have a good opportunity to flourish. Daniel prophesied about this in Daniel 9:27:

> **"And he shall confirm the covenant with many for one week: and in the midst of the week he shall cause the sacrifice and the oblation to cease, and for the overspreading of abominations he shall make** *it* **desolate, even until the consummation, and that determined shall be poured upon the desolate."**

Our Lord Himself warned about this time in the midst of the week in Matthew 24:14-16,21:

> **"And this gospel of the kingdom shall be preached in all the world for a witness unto all nations; and then shall the end come. When ye therefore shall see the abomination of desolation, spoken**

of by Daniel the prophet, stand in the holy place, (whoso readeth, let him understand:) Then let them which be in Judaea flee into the mountains: For then shall be great tribulation, such as was not since the beginning of the world to this time, no, nor ever shall be."

It is in this second half (42 months) of the tribulation that things start to gear up. The Anti-Christ is wounded to death and healed and because of this wonder the dragon (Satan) is worshipped and gives power unto the beast (Anti-Christ), who is also worshipped. It is at this point that it is given unto the Anti-Christ: **"to make war with the saints, and to overcome them: and power was given him over all kindreds, and tongues, and nations."** No wonder that our Lord warned about this time in the passage from Matthew 24 above.

Revelation 13:1–10: **"And I stood upon the sand of the sea, and saw a beast rise up out of the sea, having seven heads and ten horns, and upon his horns ten crowns, and upon his heads the name of blasphemy. And the beast which I saw was like unto a leopard, and his feet were as *the feet* of a bear, and his mouth as the mouth of a lion: and the dragon gave him his power, and his seat, and great authority. And I saw one of his heads as it were wounded to death; and his deadly wound was healed: and all the world wondered after the beast. And they worshipped the dragon which gave power unto the beast: and they worshipped the beast, saying, Who *is* like unto the beast? who is able to make war with him? And there was given unto him a mouth speaking great things and blasphemies; and power was given unto him to continue <u>forty *and* two months</u>. And he opened his mouth in blasphemy against God,**

to blaspheme his name, and his tabernacle, and them that dwell in heaven. And it was given unto him to make war with the saints, and to overcome them: and power was given him over all kindreds, and tongues, and nations. And all that dwell upon the earth shall worship him, whose names are not written in the book of life of the Lamb slain from the foundation of the world. If any man have an ear, let him hear. He that leadeth into captivity shall go into captivity: he that killeth with the sword must be killed with the sword. Here is the patience and the faith of the saints."

Shortly thereafter, a second beast comes up out of the earth who will turn out to be the false prophet in the dragon's (Satan's) attempt to duplicate the Holy Trinity with him as God the Father, the beast (Anti-Christ) as God the Son, and the second beast (false prophet) as the Holy Spirit. This second beast is described as follows:

Revelation 13:11–13: **"And I beheld another beast coming up out of the earth; and he had two horns like a lamb, and he spake as a dragon. And he exerciseth all the power of the first beast before him, and causeth the earth and them which dwell therein to worship the first beast, whose deadly wound was healed. And he doeth great wonders, so that he maketh fire come down from heaven on the earth in the sight of men."**

The second beast intensifies the **"war with the saints," "saying to them that dwell on the earth, that they should make an image to the beast,"** (Anti-Christ) and also causes all **"to receive a mark in their right hand, or in their foreheads."**

Revelation 13:14–18: **"And deceiveth them that dwell on the earth by *the means of* those miracles which he had power to do in the sight of the beast; saying to them that dwell on the earth, that they should make an image to the beast, which had the wound by a sword, and did live. And he had power to give life unto the image of the beast, that the image of the beast should both speak, and cause that as many as would not worship the image of the beast should be killed. And he causeth all, both small and great, rich and poor, free and bond, to receive a mark in their right hand, or in their foreheads: And that no man might buy or sell, save he that had the mark, or the name of the beast, or the number of his name. Here is wisdom. Let him that hath understanding count the number of the beast: for it is the number of a man; and his number *is* Six hundred threescore *and* six."**

Next, we see that the 144,000 who were sealed from the twelve tribes of Israel were **"redeemed from the earth"** and **"redeemed from among men, *being* the firstfruits unto God and to the Lamb."**

Revelation 14:1–5: **"And I looked, and, lo, a Lamb stood on the mount Sion, and with him an hundred forty *and* four thousand, having his Father's name written in their foreheads. And I heard a voice from heaven, as the voice of many waters, and as the voice of a great thunder: and I heard the voice of harpers harping with their harps: And they sung as it were a new song before the throne, and before the four beasts, and the elders: and no man could learn that song but the hundred *and* forty *and* four thousand, which were redeemed from the earth. These are they**

**which were not defiled with women; for they are
virgins. These are they which follow the Lamb
whithersoever he goeth. These were redeemed
from among men,** *being* **the firstfruits unto God
and to the Lamb. And in their mouth was found
no guile: for they are without fault before the
throne of God.''**

Concerning the Anti-Christ, it was earlier learned that
at this time **"power was given unto him to continue
forty** *and* **two months"** and **"it was given unto him to
make war with the saints, and to overcome them: and
power was given him over all kindreds, and tongues,
and nations."** With the coming of the false prophet, we
saw the war intensify with the image of the beast and
the mark of the beast. We also saw earlier that the two
witnesses were ascended to heaven and now the 144,000
are **"redeemed from the earth"** and are in heaven. We
don't know for sure if the 144,000 were killed by the war
or if they were caught up to heaven by God, but either
way it would almost look like God is going to be without
a witness on earth soon. We don't have to wait long to see
God using the angels for another important mission: to
preach to the entire earth.

Revelation 14:6–13: **"And I saw another angel
fly in the midst of heaven, having the everlasting
gospel to preach unto them that dwell on the
earth, and to every nation, and kindred, and
tongue, and people, Saying with a loud voice,
Fear God, and give glory to him; for the hour
of his judgment is come: and worship him that
made heaven, and earth, and the sea, and the
fountains of waters. And there followed another
angel, saying, Babylon is fallen, is fallen, that
great city, because she made all nations drink
of the wine of the wrath of her fornication. And**

the third angel followed them, saying with a loud voice, If any man worship the beast and his image, and receive *his* mark in his forehead, or in his hand, The same shall drink of the wine of the wrath of God, which is poured out without mixture into the cup of his indignation; and he shall be tormented with fire and brimstone in the presence of the holy angels, and in the presence of the Lamb: And the smoke of their torment ascendeth up for ever and ever: and they have no rest day nor night, who worship the beast and his image, and whosoever receiveth the mark of his name. Here is the patience of the saints: here are they that keep the commandments of God, and the faith of Jesus. And I heard a voice from heaven saying unto me, Write, Blessed *are* the dead which die in the Lord from henceforth: Yea, saith the Spirit, that they may rest from their labours; and their works do follow them."

By now the seven seals have been opened and the seven trumpets have been sounded. If you go to your Bible and review them, you will notice that the judgments associated with the seals and trumpets, as awesome as they are, will not measure up to the escalation of God's wrath represented by the last series of judgments, called the seven vials. It appears that the vials are poured out during the last half (42 months) of the tribulation. No wonder the stern warning was given by our Lord in Matthew 24 to those who would still be alive at this time and are trying to resist the Anti-Christ with all his devices. After the pouring out of the last of the seven vials, the earthly seat of the Anti-Christ and his associates of doom, the city of Babylon, is destroyed in one hour:

Revelation 18:17–19: **"For in one hour so great riches is come to nought. And every shipmaster,**

> and all the company in ships, and sailors, and as many as trade by sea, stood afar off, And cried when they saw the smoke of her burning, saying, What *city is* like unto this great city! And they cast dust on their heads, and cried, weeping and wailing, saying, Alas, alas, that great city, wherein were made rich all that had ships in the sea by reason of her costliness! for in one hour is she made desolate."

We learn in Revelation 16:12–16:

> "And the sixth angel poured out his vial upon the great river Euphrates; and the water thereof was dried up, that the way of the kings of the east might be prepared. And I saw three unclean spirits like frogs *come* out of the mouth of the dragon, and out of the mouth of the beast, and out of the mouth of the false prophet. For they are the spirits of devils, working miracles, *which* go forth unto the kings of the earth and of the whole world, to gather them to the battle of that great day of God Almighty. Behold, I come as a thief. Blessed *is* he that watcheth, and keepeth his garments, lest he walk naked, and they see his shame. And he gathered them together into a place called in the Hebrew tongue Armageddon."

According to the verses above there are three unclean spirits that come out of the mouths of the unholy, counterfeit trinity in one last effort to defeat God in what is known popularly as the *battle of Armageddon*. Details of this famous future battle are given in two places in the book of Revelation:

Revelation 14:14–20: **"And I looked, and behold a white cloud, and upon the cloud *one* sat like** unto the Son of man, having on his head a golden crown, and in his hand a sharp sickle. And another angel came out of the temple, crying with a loud voice to him that sat on the cloud, Thrust in thy sickle, and reap: for the time is come for thee to reap; for the harvest of the earth is ripe. And he that sat on the cloud thrust in his sickle on the earth; and the earth was reaped. And another angel came out of the temple which is in heaven, he also having a sharp sickle. And another angel came out from the altar, which had power over fire; and cried with a loud cry to him that had the sharp sickle, saying, Thrust in thy sharp sickle, and gather the clusters of the vine of the earth; for her grapes are fully ripe. And the angel thrust in his sickle into the earth, and gathered the vine of the earth, and cast *it* into the great winepress of the wrath of God. And the winepress was trodden without the city, and blood came out of the winepress, even unto the horse bridles, by the space of a thousand *and* six hundred furlongs."

Revelation 19:11–21: **"And I saw heaven opened, and behold a white horse; and he that sat upon him *was* called Faithful and True, and in righteousness he doth judge and make war. His eyes *were* as a flame of fire, and on his head *were* many crowns; and he had a name written, that no man knew, but he himself. And he *was* clothed with a vesture dipped in blood: and his name is called The Word of God. And the armies *which were* in heaven followed him upon white horses, clothed in fine linen, white and clean. And out of his mouth goeth a sharp sword, that with it he should smite the nations: and he shall rule them with a rod of iron: and he treadeth the winepress** of the fierceness and wrath of Almighty God. And he hath on *his* vesture and on his thigh a name written, KING OF KINGS, AND LORD OF LORDS. And I saw an angel standing in the sun; and he cried with a loud voice, saying to all the fowls that fly in the midst of heaven, Come and gather yourselves together unto the supper of the great God; That ye may eat the flesh of kings, and the flesh of captains, and the flesh of mighty men, and the flesh of horses, and of them that sit on them, and the flesh of all *men, both* free and bond, both small and great. And I saw the beast, and the kings of the earth, and their armies, gathered together to make war against him that sat on the horse, and against his army. And the beast was taken, and with him the false prophet that wrought miracles before him, with which he deceived them that had received the mark of the beast, and them that worshipped his image. These both were cast alive into a lake of fire burning with brimstone. And the remnant were slain with the sword of him that sat upon the horse, which *sword* proceeded out of his mouth: and all the fowls were filled with their flesh."

As we learn from the last few verses above, the beast (Anti-Christ) and the false prophet were cast alive into the lake of fire, and next, we learn what happens to the dragon (Satan).

Revelation 20:1–3: **"And I saw an angel come down from heaven, having the key of the bottomless pit and a great chain in his hand. And he laid hold on the dragon, that old serpent, which is the Devil, and Satan, and bound him a thousand years, And cast him into the bottomless**

pit, and shut him up, and set a seal upon him, that he should deceive the nations no more, till the thousand years should be fulfilled: and after that he must be loosed a little season."

So let's review: the Anti-Christ and the false prophet are out of the way in the lake of fire, the dragon (Satan) is shut up in the bottomless pit for a thousand years, and the remnant (the kings of the earth and their armies) has been slain in the *battle of Armageddon*. The Lord Jesus Christ is now standing on earth, victorious, with the armies of heaven and anyone who has survived to this point on earth. Meanwhile, in heaven, there is a large number of souls who were killed in the tribulation about whom we read in Revelation 20:4:

" . . . and I *saw* the souls of them that were beheaded for the witness of Jesus, and for the word of God, and which had not worshipped the beast, neither his image, neither had received *his* mark upon their foreheads, or in their hands; and they lived and reigned with Christ a thousand years." We also read in Revelation 20:5,6: **"But the rest of the dead lived not again until the thousand years were finished. This *is* the first resurrection. Blessed and holy *is* he that hath part in the first resurrection: on such the second death hath no power, but they shall be priests of God and of Christ, and shall reign with him a thousand years."**

Based on this passage and other passages of Scripture, which we will also look at, I believe that all the saved of all ages (other than we in the body of Christ) will have their part in this first resurrection to go into the long-awaited kingdom without end (see Luke 1:31–33 below), and in the first phase, reign with Christ for a thousand years.

Let's list some Scriptural references for the kingdom and then we will go on to see just how that long-awaited kingdom will be set up.

> Exodus 19:5,6: **"Now therefore, if ye will obey my voice indeed, and keep my covenant, then ye shall be a peculiar treasure unto me above all people: for all the earth *is* mine: And ye shall be unto me a kingdom of priests, and an holy nation. These *are* the words which thou shalt speak unto the children of Israel."**

> II Samuel 7:8–17: **"Now therefore so shalt thou say unto my servant David, Thus saith the LORD of hosts, I took thee from the sheepcote, from following the sheep, to be ruler over my people, over Israel: And I was with thee whithersoever thou wentest, and have cut off all thine enemies out of thy sight, and have made thee a great name, like unto the name of the great *men* that *are* in the earth. Moreover I will appoint a place for my people Israel, and will plant them, that they may dwell in a place of their own, and move no more; neither shall the children of wickedness afflict them any more, as beforetime, And as since the time that I commanded judges *to be* over my people Israel, and have caused thee to rest from all thine enemies. Also the LORD telleth thee that he will make thee an house. And when thy days be fulfilled, and thou shalt sleep with thy fathers, I will set up thy seed after thee, which shall proceed out of thy bowels, and I will establish his kingdom. He shall build an house for my name, and I will stablish the throne of his kingdom for ever. I will be his father, and he shall be my son. If he commit iniquity, I will chasten him with the rod of men, and with the**

stripes of the children of men: But my mercy shall not depart away from him, as I took *it* from Saul, whom I put away before thee. And thine house and thy kingdom shall be established for ever before thee: thy throne shall be established for ever. According to all these words, and according to all this vision, so did Nathan speak unto David."

Isaiah 9:6,7: "For unto us a child is born, unto us a son is given: and the government shall be upon his shoulder: and his name shall be called Wonderful, Counsellor, The mighty God, The everlasting Father, The Prince of Peace. Of the increase of *his* government and peace *there shall be* no end, upon the throne of David, and upon his kingdom, to order it, and to establish it with judgment and with justice from henceforth even for ever. The zeal of the LORD of hosts will perform this."

Matthew 3:1,2: "In those days came John the Baptist, preaching in the wilderness of Judaea, And saying, Repent ye: for the kingdom of heaven is at hand."

Matthew 4:17: "From that time Jesus began to preach, and to say, Repent: for the kingdom of heaven is at hand."

Matthew 10:5–7: "These twelve Jesus sent forth, and commanded them, saying, Go not into the way of the Gentiles, and into *any* city of the Samaritans enter ye not: But go rather to the lost sheep of the house of Israel. And as ye go, preach, saying, The kingdom of heaven is at hand."

Mark 1:14,15: **"Now after that John was put in prison, Jesus came into Galilee, preaching the gospel of the kingdom of God, And saying, The time is fulfilled, and the kingdom of God is at hand: repent ye, and believe the gospel."**

Luke 1:31–33: **"And, behold, thou shalt conceive in thy womb, and bring forth a son, and shalt call his name JESUS. He shall be great, and shall be called the Son of the Highest: and the Lord God shall give unto him the throne of his father David: And he shall reign over the house of Jacob for ever; and of his kingdom there shall be no end."**

Acts 2:29,30: **"Men *and* brethren, let me freely speak unto you of the patriarch David, that he is both dead and buried, and his sepulchre is with us unto this day. Therefore being a prophet, and knowing that God had sworn with an oath to him, that of the fruit of his loins, according to the flesh, he would raise up Christ to sit on his throne."**

Acts 3:19–21: **"Repent ye therefore, and be converted, that your sins may be blotted out, when the times of refreshing shall come from the presence of the Lord; And he shall send Jesus Christ, which before was preached unto you: Whom the heaven must receive until the times of restitution of all things, which God hath spoken by the mouth of all his holy prophets since the world began."**

That last passage from Acts 3:19–21 is the first actual offer of the kingdom to Israel by the Apostle Peter after the day of Pentecost. We know, however, that during the events of the ninth chapter of Acts, the kingdom program was being put on hold, and was being interrupted by the current *mystery* program.

There is some interesting prophecy in the book of Daniel that involves the numbering of days:

> Daniel 12:11–13: **"And from the time *that* the daily *sacrifice* shall be taken away, and the abomination that maketh desolate set up, *there shall be* a thousand two hundred and ninety days. Blessed *is* he that waiteth, and cometh to the thousand three hundred and five and thirty days. But go thou thy way till the end *be:* for thou shalt rest, and stand in thy lot at the end of the days."**

The first numbering is 1,290 days that would add 30 days to the 1,260 days of the last half of the tribulation. The second numbering is 1,335 days that would add an additional 45 days to the 1,290 days, or 75 days in total. Let's see if Scripture gives some light on what will happen during those extra days. The first passage, I believe, describes the judgment of Israel, which will last 30 days and involve all Jews who survive to the end of the tribulation.

> Ezekiel 20:33–38: **"*As* I live, saith the Lord GOD, surely with a mighty hand, and with a stretched out arm, and with fury poured out, will I rule over you: And I will bring you out from the people, and will gather you out of the countries wherein ye are scattered, with a mighty hand, and with a stretched out arm, and with fury poured out. And I will bring you into the wilderness of the people, and there will I plead with you face to face. Like as I pleaded with your fathers in the wilderness of the land of Egypt, so will I plead with you, saith the Lord GOD. And I will cause**

> you to pass under the rod, and I will bring you
> into the bond of the covenant: And I will purge
> out from among you the rebels, and them that
> transgress against me: I will bring them forth
> out of the country where they sojourn, and they
> shall not enter into the land of Israel: and ye
> shall know that I *am* the LORD."

The next passage, I believe, describes the judgment of
the nations, which will last 45 days and involve all the
Gentile nations that survive the tribulation. The sheep are
the nations that helped Israel and the goats are the nations
that didn't help Israel during the tribulation.

> Matthew 25:31–46: **"When the Son of man shall
> come in his glory, and all the holy angels with
> him, then shall he sit upon the throne of his glory:
> And before him shall be gathered all nations:
> and he shall separate them one from another,
> as a shepherd divideth *his* sheep from the goats:
> And he shall set the sheep on his right hand, but
> the goats on the left. Then shall the King say
> unto them on his right hand, Come, ye blessed
> of my Father, inherit the kingdom prepared
> for you from the foundation of the world: For
> I was an hungred, and ye gave me meat: I was
> thirsty, and ye gave me drink: I was a stranger,
> and ye took me in: Naked, and ye clothed me:
> I was sick, and ye visited me: I was in prison,
> and ye came unto me. Then shall the righteous
> answer him, saying, Lord, when saw we thee an
> hungred, and fed *thee?* or thirsty, and gave *thee*
> drink? When saw we thee a stranger, and took
> *thee* in? or naked, and clothed *thee?* Or when
> saw we thee sick, or in prison, and came unto
> thee? And the King shall answer and say unto
> them, Verily I say unto you, Inasmuch as ye have**

done *it* unto one of the least of these my brethren, ye have done *it* unto me. Then shall he say also unto them on the left hand, Depart from me, ye cursed, into everlasting fire, prepared for the devil and his angels: For I was an hungred, and ye gave me no meat: I was thirsty, and ye gave me no drink: I was a stranger, and ye took me not in: naked, and ye clothed me not: sick, and in prison, and ye visited me not. Then shall they also answer him, saying, Lord, when saw we thee an hungred, or athirst, or a stranger, or naked, or sick, or in prison, and did not minister unto thee? Then shall he answer them, saying, Verily I say unto you, Inasmuch as ye did *it* not to one of the least of these, ye did *it* not to me. And these shall go away into everlasting punishment: but the righteous into life eternal."

The first phase of the kingdom, 1,000 years, is now set up and the kingdom saints of all ages are resurrected to go into the promised kingdom. This includes, of course, the Twelve Apostles who will sit on twelve thrones judging the twelve tribes of Israel. Let's look at some Scriptures along with some comments.

Job 19:25,26: **"For I know *that* my redeemer liveth, and *that* he shall stand at the latter *day* upon the earth: And *though* after my skin *worms* destroy this *body,* yet in my flesh shall I see God."**

Job possessed an earthly hope of being resurrected in his flesh.

Isaiah 2:2–4: **"And it shall come to pass in the last days, *that* the mountain of the LORD's house shall be established in the top of the mountains, and shall be exalted above the hills; and all** nations shall flow unto it. And many people shall go and say, Come ye, and let us go up to the mountain of the LORD, to the house of the God of Jacob; and he will teach us of his ways, and we will walk in his paths: for out of Zion shall go forth the law, and the word of the LORD from Jerusalem. And he shall judge among the nations, and shall rebuke many people: and they shall beat their swords into plowshares, and their spears into pruninghooks: nation shall not lift up sword against nation, neither shall they learn war any more."

Jeremiah 31:31–34: "Behold, the days come, saith the LORD, that I will make a new covenant with the house of Israel, and with the house of Judah: Not according to the covenant that I made with their fathers in the day *that* I took them by the hand to bring them out of the land of Egypt; which my covenant they brake, although I was an husband unto them, saith the LORD: But this *shall be* the covenant that I will make with the house of Israel; After those days, saith the LORD, I will put my law in their inward parts, and write it in their hearts; and will be their God, and they shall be my people. And they shall teach no more every man his neighbour, and every man his brother, saying, Know the LORD: for they shall all know me, from the least of them unto the greatest of them, saith the LORD; for I will forgive their iniquity, and I will remember their sin no more."

Daniel 12:1,2: "And at that time shall Michael stand up, the great prince which standeth for the children of thy people: and there shall be a time of trouble, such as never was since there was a nation *even* to that same time: and at that time thy people shall be delivered, every one that shall be found written in the book. And many of them that sleep in the dust of the earth shall awake, some to everlasting life, and some to shame *and* everlasting contempt."

It should be understood that there are 1,000 years between "some to everlasting life," and "some to shame *and* everlasting contempt."

Matthew 19:28: "And Jesus said unto them, Verily I say unto you, That ye which have followed me, in the regeneration when the Son of man shall sit in the throne of his glory, ye also shall sit upon twelve thrones, judging the twelve tribes of Israel."

Luke 22:29,30: "And I appoint unto you a kingdom, as my Father hath appointed unto me; That ye may eat and drink at my table in my kingdom, and sit on thrones judging the twelve tribes of Israel."

John 5:25–29: "Verily, verily, I say unto you, The hour is coming, and now is, when the dead shall hear the voice of the Son of God: and they that hear shall live. For as the Father hath life in himself; so hath he given to the Son to have life in himself; And hath given him authority to execute judgment also, because he is the Son of man. Marvel not at this: for the hour is coming, in the which all that are in the graves shall hear his voice, And shall come forth; they that have done good, unto the resurrection of life; and they that have done evil, unto the resurrection of damnation."

Here again, it should be understood that there are 1,000 years between **"the resurrection of life"** and **"the resurrection of damnation."**

At the end of the thousand year reign of Christ on earth, unbelievably, sin will for the final time increase in the earth. This time God will quickly end this final outbreak of sin in what is known as the battle of Gog and Magog.

> Revelation 20:7–9: **"And when the thousand years are expired, Satan shall be loosed out of his prison, And shall go out to deceive the nations which are in the four quarters of the earth, Gog and Magog, to gather them together to battle: the number of whom *is* as the sand of the sea. And they went up on the breadth of the earth, and compassed the camp of the saints about, and the beloved city: and fire came down from God out of heaven, and devoured them."**

The devil is dealt with and the lost of all ages are resurrected and given the final judgment of God from the *great white throne.*

> Revelation 20:10–15: **"And the devil that deceived them was cast into the lake of fire and brimstone, where the beast and the false prophet *are,* and shall be tormented day and night for ever and ever. And I saw a great white throne, and him that sat on it, from whose face the earth and the heaven fled away; and there was found no place for them. And I saw the dead, small and great, stand before God; and the books were opened: and another book was opened, which is *the book* of life: and the dead were judged out of those things which were written in the books, according to their works. And the sea gave up the dead which were in it; and death and hell**

delivered up the dead which were in them: and they were judged every man according to their works. And death and hell were cast into the lake of fire. This is the second death. And whosoever was not found written in the book of life was cast into the lake of fire."

Let's pause for a final review. The last review ended with a large number of souls in heaven who had died in the tribulation. We then saw the first phase of the kingdom being set up with the judgment of Israel first, followed by the judgment of the nations, then the first resurrection of the kingdom saints of all ages to go into the kingdom. The kingdom begins and at the end of 1,000 years Satan is loosed, causes the final rebellion, is defeated, and cast into the lake of fire. Then, there is a second resurrection of the lost of all ages to face the great white throne and their final judgment, which is that all of them are cast into the lake of fire.

The last two chapters in the book of Revelation describe the eternal state where all kingdom saints and all members of the body of Christ will live in a loving family relationship with God the Father, the Lord Jesus Christ, and the Holy Spirit in a new heaven, a new earth, and a new Jerusalem. Read those two chapters prayerfully, with thanksgiving, as they will describe your reward for believing the gospel of the grace of God, which is that Christ died for your sins, was buried, and rose again the third day. Praise God!

I will close with a few verses from Paul's letters to the church, which is His body.

Ephesians 2:7: **"That in the ages to come he might shew the exceeding riches of his grace in *his* kindness toward us through Christ Jesus."**

I Corinthians 2:9: **"But as it is written, Eye hath not seen, nor ear heard, neither have entered into the heart of man, the things which God hath prepared for them that love him."**

II Corinthians 4:17: **"For our light affliction, which is but for a moment, worketh for us a far more exceeding *and* eternal weight of glory."**

The two charts in Appendixes I and II will help you to evaluate whether or not you have come to an understanding of the material in this book. The first chart is a simplified version of the second one. You may have to reread[14] all or parts of this book to follow all the significance of both charts. I think you will find that what you gain by doing so will be well worth the effort. Appendix III is a collection of thoughts to travel from Denominationalism to The Word Rightly Divided. Appendix IV is a chart listing the major events in the book of Revelation in chronological order. Following Appendix IV is a handy Bible Index listing page numbers for all Scripture references in this book.

My prayer for you is twofold: one, that the foundation you have built by taking the time to read and understand this book will lead to tremendous Spiritual growth for you; and two, now that you're armed with what this book has added to your knowledge of His will, that you will have the confidence to share the good news and simplicity of the gospel of the grace of God when the Holy Spirit leads you. May you follow His Spirit in all that you do!

---

[14] François Mauriac: "If you would tell me the heart of a man, tell me not what he reads but what he rereads."

APPENDIX I

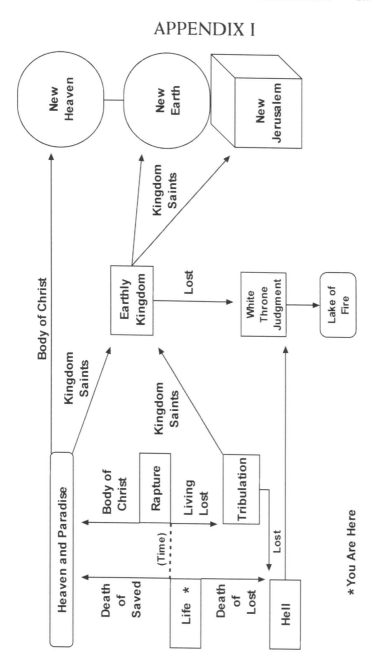

APPENDIX II

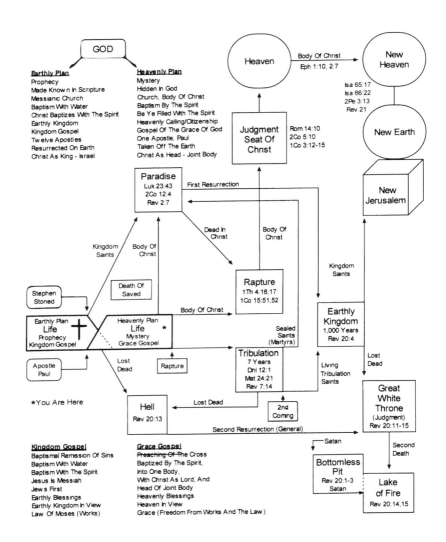

Earthly Plan
Prophecy
Made Known In Scripture
Messianic Church
Baptism With Water
Christ Baptizes With The Spirit
Earthly Kingdom
Kingdom Gospel
Twelve Apostles
Resurrected On Earth
Christ As King - Israel

Heavenly Plan
Mystery
Hidden In God
Church, Body Of Christ
Baptism By The Spirit
Be Ye Filled With The Spirit
Heavenly Calling/Citizenship
Gospel Of The Grace Of God
One Apostle, Paul
Taken Off The Earth
Christ As Head - Joint Body

★You Are Here

Kingdom Gospel
Baptismal Remission Of Sins
Baptism With Water
Baptism With The Spirit
Jesus Is Messiah
Jews First
Earthly Blessings
Earthly Kingdom In View
Law Of Moses (Works)

Grace Gospel
Preaching Of The Cross
Baptized By The Spirit,
Into One Body,
With Christ As Lord, And
Head Of Joint Body
Heavenly Blessings
Heaven In View
Grace (Freedom From Works And The Law)

APPENDIX III

Stepping Stones to Travel from Denominationalism to The Word Rightly Divided

The Church the Body of Christ Began in Mid-Acts with Paul

Paul was the First to Preach the Gospel of the Grace of God

Apostle Paul's Ministry was Distinctive from that of the Twelve Apostles

Paul Received the Mystery from Christ by Direct Heavenly Revelation

God Temporarily Set Aside Israel in Mid-Acts as they Reject their Messiah

Water Baptism Stems from the O.T. Rite of Cleansing for the Priesthood

Kingdom Gospel: Prelude to Establishing Earthly Kingdom with Israel

God's Will includes an Earthly Plan and a Heavenly Plan

The Word Rightly Divided

Prophecy Divided from Mystery
Church and Israel Distinct
Premillennialism
Pretribulational Rapture
Futurist
Mid-Acts Position
Church Distinct
Pauline Authority
Grace Enthroned

Denominationalism

Acts 2 Position
No Rapture
Partial Rapture
Midtribulationalism
Postmillennialism
Amillennialism
Church and Israel Confused
Prophecy and Mystery Mixed

The Most Important Division in the Bible is between Prophecy and Mystery ©

APPENDIX IV

Passage	Events And Items In Chronological Order In The Book Of Revelation
Rev 11:3-12	Power Is Given To Two Witnesses To Prophesy 1,260 Days
Rev 7:4	144,000 Sealed From All Of The Tribes Of The Children Of Israel (12,000 x 12)
Rev 1:2,4	John Writes The Prophecy Of The Things He Saw Unto The Seven Churches* In Asia
Rev 6,8	Seven Seal Judgments Opened By The Lamb
Rev 8:2	Seven Angels Given Seven Trumpets
Rev 12:9	Great Dragon (Old Serpent, Devil, Satan Which Deceives The Whole World) Cast To Earth With His Angels
Rev 12:14	Woman Given Wings To Fly Into Wilderness And Is Nourished For Three And One Half Years (1,260 Days)
Rev 13:5	Power And A Mouth Given To Beast Speaking Great Things And Blasphemies For 42 Months (1,260 Days)
Rev 13:12	Second Beast Has The Power Of First Beast And Causes Those Dwelling On Earth To Worship First Beast
Rev 13:14	Second Beast Deceives Them On Earth Saying They Should Make An Image To The Beast
Rev 13:15	Second Beast Gives Life To Image To Speak And Cause Any Not Worshipping First Beast To Be Killed
Rev 13:16	Second Beast Causes All To Receive Mark In Right Hand Or Forehead To Buy Or Sell
Rev 14:6	Angel Preaches Everlasting Gospel On Earth
Rev 14:8	Angel Saying Babylon Is Fallen
Rev 15:7	One Of Four Beasts Give Seven Angels Seven Golden Vials Full Of The Wrath Of God
Rev 1:7	Jesus Christ Comes With Clouds - Every Eye Sees Him Also They Who Pierced Him And All Shall Wail
Rev 19:11-14	Jesus Christ Comes To Earth With The Armies Of Heaven All On White Horses
Rev 19:15-19	The Battle (Armageddon) Ensues Against The Beast And The Kings Of The Earth
Rev 19:20,21	Beast And False Prophet Cast Alive Into Lake Of Fire - Remnant Slain With Sword Of Jesus Christ
Rev 20:1	Angel Comes Down From Heaven With Key Of Bottomless Pit And A Great Chain In His Hand
Rev 20:2,3	Angel Laid Hold On Satan And Bound Him For A Thousand Years And Cast Him Into Bottomless Pit
Rev 20:3	After The Thousand Years Satan Must Be Loosed A Little Season (While)
Rev 20:4	Souls Which Were Beheaded For The Witness Of Jesus And God Which:
Rev 20:4	Had Not Worshipped The Beast His Image Or Had His Mark Lived
Rev 20:4	These Souls Reigned With Christ A Thousand Years
Rev 20:6	Blessed And Holy Is He In The First Resurrection On Such The Second Death Has No Power
Rev 20:6	Those In First Resurrection Shall Be Priests And Shall Reign With Christ A Thousand Years
Rev 19:7-9	Marriage Supper Of The Lamb
Rev 20:7	When The Thousand Years Are Expired Satan Shall Be Loosed Out Of His Prison
Rev 20:8	He Will Go Out To Deceive The Nations In The Four Quarters Of The Earth
Rev 20:8	Those Deceived Are Gathered Together To Battle The Number Of Whom Is As The Sand Of The Sea
Rev 20:9	They Went Up And Compassed The Camp Of The Saints And The Beloved City
Rev 20:9	Fire Came Down From God Out Of Heaven And Devoured Them
Rev 20:10	The Devil Cast Into The Lake Of Fire Where The Beast And False Prophet Are
Rev 20:11	John Saw Great White Throne And Him That Sat On It From Whose Face Earth And Heaven Fled Away
Rev 20:12	The Dead Small And Great From The Sea The Grave And Hell Stand Before God
Rev 20:13	The Dead Were Judged Out Of The Book Of Life And Other Books According To Their Works
Rev 20:14,15	Death Hell And Whosoever Not Found In The Book Of Life Cast Into The Lake Of Fire - Second Death
Rev 21:1	John Saw A New Heaven And A New Earth - First Earth Passed Away And There Was No More Sea
Rev 21:2	John Saw The Holy City New Jerusalem Coming Down From God Out Of Heaven Prepared As A Bride
*	" Churches" in the context is taken to mean kingdom churches with kingdom saints

BIBLE INDEX

ENDNOTES

[1]Cornelius R. Stam, *Things That Differ,* page 20.

[2]Berean Bible Society, for additional literature: (262)255–4750, www.bereanbiblesociety.org

[3]Grace Bible College, TH 414–(adapted excerpt from) *Studies in Dispensational Theology,* T. F. Conklin, Course Prof., Spring 1994

[4]Some would take this as meaning that when Christ returns in the *rapture,* the gifts will be done away. Neither the Greek word for *perfect,* which is neuter, nor the sentence structure supports this idea. We would have found "when He who is perfect" rather than "when that which is perfect."

[5]We know that the Lord's earthly ministry began when He was about thirty and our dating is off by perhaps four years. Luke 3:23: **"And Jesus himself began to be about thirty years of age,"**

[6]Kingdom *of* heaven is taken to mean coming *from* heaven (to earth).

[7]The dimension of *love* (it's the pinnacle) will be dealt with, in detail, in Book Two.

[8]Gr, *pleroma:* completion

[9]Isn't it sobering to think that the *rapture* could happen as you are leading someone to Christ, the moment they believe, and isn't it also sobering to think that once the

rapture occurs, you will lose the opportunity to talk to your friends and family about trusting Christ?

[10]This word appears to have a dual meaning, it's used one other time in Acts 21:21: "**. . . thou teachest all the Jews which are among the Gentiles to <u>forsake</u> Moses . . .**" it carries the idea of *depart* (from Moses). Many translations also use *apostasy* or *rebellion* in II Thessalonians 2:3.

[11]Acts 17:11 **"These [Bereans] were more noble than those in Thessalonica, in that they received the word with all readiness of mind, and searched the scriptures daily, whether those things were so."**

[12]The word *gospel* is best not used alone but along with *kingdom* or *grace of God* to show which gospel is being referred to, i.e., the gospel of the kingdom or the gospel of the grace of God.

[13]When Peter went to Cornelius in Acts 10 he was on a special mission, to Gentiles, and didn't go because Israel was converted and wasn't moving out based on the Great Commission.

[14]François Mauriac: "If you would tell me the heart of a man, tell me not what he reads but what he rereads."

Contact Fred Lewis
Email: fredlewis@biblicaladvancedbasics.com
Online: www.biblicaladvancedbasics.com

ORDER INFORMATION

To order additional copies of this book, please visit
www.redemption-press.com.
Also available on Amazon.com and BarnesandNoble.com
Or by calling toll free 1-844-2REDEEM.